RUSSIAN RESEARCH CENTER STUDIES, 47

THE NEW FACE OF SOVIET TOTALITARIANISM

ADAM B. ULAM

THE NEW FACE
OF SOVIET TOTALITARIANISM

HARVARD UNIVERSITY PRESS

CAMBRIDGE, MASSACHUSETTS | 1963

The Russian Research Center of Harvard University is
supported by grants from the Carnegie Corporation,
the Ford Foundation, and the Rockefeller Foundation.
The Center carries out interdisciplinary study of Russian institutions and behavior and related subjects.

This volume was prepared in part under a grant from
the Carnegie Corporation of New York. That Corporation is not, however, the author, owner, publisher,
or proprietor of the publication and is not to be
understood as approving by virtue of its grant any
of the statements made or views expressed therein.

ACKNOWLEDGMENTS

My thanks are due to the editors of *World Politics,* to Harvard University Press, and to Yale University Press for permission to use essays which previously appeared under their auspices. My essay on Soviet historiography was delivered originally before the Conference on Soviet Historiography in Geneva in July 1961 which was organized by the Congress for Cultural Freedom, and I am grateful to the officials of the Congress for permission to include it in this book. The introductory and concluding essays are printed for the first time.

It would take me too long to list all the persons, most of them associated with the Russian Research Center at Harvard, who have helped me with advice and criticism, but I am bound to express my debt to Professor Merle Fainsod and my former secretary, Miss Mary Towle. I owe a great deal to the editorial assistance of Mrs. Alan Lebowitz of Harvard University Press.

CONTENTS

THE NEW FACE OF SOVIET TOTALITARIANISM

INTRODUCTION

The student of Soviet affairs has every reason to sympathize with the Russian poet of long ago when he sang that "by reason alone you cannot hope to comprehend Russia." And when the poet Tyutchev concludes that this understanding must come only through an act of faith, the modern writer can only sigh and regret the advantages which poetry has over politics.

For indeed reason or, to write more meaningfully, scholarship can but imperfectly illuminate the recent history of the Soviet Union. The scholar is at the mercy of his materials, and in the case of Russia the materials bearing on politics are not only inadequate but often of a deceptive or ambiguous character. The essays which follow bear witness to this fact. When the chapter entitled "The New Face of Soviet Totalitarianism" was written, our knowledge of the dramatic events of June 1957 was based on the revelations made at the plenum of the Central Committee in December 1958 and at the Twenty-First Party Congress in January 1959. But at the Twenty-Second Party Congress in October 1961 Khrushchev told a more detailed and in some ways different story of the challenge to his power in June 1957. The analysis contained here in the last chapter tries to unravel that evidence, yet it is obvious that the last word has not been said.

The secretive habits of the masters of Russia are but a part of the trouble. A greater source of confusion is found in their assumption that history is simply a part of politics and that it should always be at the service of the party, that is, at the service of those who rule the party at the given moment. Communism more than any other movement has been conscious of its historical role and its leaders avid in their historical pretensions. Stalin, whose figure dominates the Soviet scene of the last forty years (and it will take more than the ejection of his remains from the Mausoleum or the renaming of cities to erase this domination), conceived his historical role with a naive yet awesome self-consciousness. Son of a Georgian cobbler, he saw himself as the greatest in the line of the despot builders of the Russian empire. The memoirs of the famous film actor Cherkassov record Stalin's helpful hints to him when he was to portray the role of Ivan the Terrible. This crowned psychopath was for Stalin a great statesman, the unifier of Muscovy. Two aspects of Ivan's personality and career drew Stalin's rebuke: his failure to extirpate the rival princely families and the mad tyrant's intermittent bouts of religious repentance for his frightful bloodbaths. It is not difficult to draw conclusions from Stalin's historical "critique" of Ivan. The Communist tyrant in massacring the party hierarchy must have felt that he was obviating the danger of a "Time of Troubles" like the one which swept Russia not long after Ivan's death, and *he* is not on record as expressing any regret or repentance for the terror which dwarfs even Ivan's Oprichnina.

This kind of self-consciousness has had dire results for the writing of history. The Communist leaders have always felt the need, and the tendency is both older and longer-lasting than Stalin's rule, to remold the past in terms of the political needs of the present. If the beginnings of the Russian state have to be presented from a "correct" political point of view, what hope is there for an objective or even very informative story of the intraparty struggle in 1957? Take the rapidly changing official image of Marshal Voroshilov. Until October 1961 he had been a revered elder statesman of Communism. At the Twenty-Second Party Congress he was "revealed" as an active participant in Stalin's crimes and one of the main intriguers in the party crisis of 1957. A few more weeks and the image of an erstwhile hero, then a criminal, was allowed to subside as one of an old man, who, true, has made some mistakes, but who has also "rendered great services to the Soviet people."

One wonders whether even in the mind of the present-day leaders there exists a clear and coherent picture of their own role and behavior during Stalin's reign. And if by any chance there are people who have a lucid recall of their previous political incarnations, there can be, alas, little doubt that much of the documentation of those years has been irretrievably destroyed. Will a future historian be able to find "uncorrected" minutes of the Politburo meetings of the thirties and forties? In my essay on Soviet historiography it is recounted how, following Stalin's death, some previously lost documents mysteriously found their way back into the party archives. But it is unreasonable to hope for too much. The Twenty-Second Party Congress decided to build a monument to the victims of the purges. If the party ever gets around to doing it, historical truth should be included among the list of casualties.

The paucity and falsification of the documentation on the Soviet side are but one of the major difficulties confronted by a Western scholar. From the time the first English travelers appeared in Muscovy, the subject of Russia has been veiled in Western literature by an aura of exoticism and strangeness. When the tsars' Empire emerged as one of the Great Powers, the paradox of its autocratic institutions amidst a Europe progressing, so it seemed in those days, toward constitution-alism and democracy only enhanced the view that Russia was "different." The prosaic ways of scholarship, of statistics, of the study of comparative institutions, more often than not were discarded for the more exhilarating if obscurantist discussions of the "Russian soul," of the moujik and of the Tatar nature which slumbered in every Russian. Even today much of the discussion of the Bolshevik period is marred by a lack of awareness that pre-1914 Russia was not only the country of Dostoyevskian characters, of political oppression and pogroms, but also one of the leaders of Europe in the arts and sciences; that for a generation before the revolution industry was grow-ing by leaps and bounds; that, for all the inherent political limitations, the tsarist bureaucracy and judiciary scored a number of impressive achievements; and that the brief period of limited constitutionalism after 1906 gave to the Russian citizen more freedom and legal protection than he was to know even during the most "liberal" interludes of the Soviet rule.

With the Communist period, the discussion of Russia took on another complication. To the alleged exoticism of the country was added the challenge of its political system with its mission-ary character and world-wide ambitions. A Frenchman or an American writing about the USSR and Communism would be writing not only about a country and an ideology; he would also be expressing his approval or disapproval of his own country and his own tradition. To many in the West, and the talk is now not of the Communists or fellow travelers, Soviet Russia was seen through the distorting prism of the Great Depression, of the challenge of fascism or the partnership in the war against Hitler. Today, when the Communists them-selves offer abundant and horrifying evidence of how deep and widespread were the ravages of Stalinism, it is a sad recol-lection that one of the best books on Russia written in that period, Sir John Maynard's *Russia in Flux,* could assert that the purges of the thirties affected just a small group at the top and were not felt by the great mass of the Soviet people.

Disillusionment is no better foundation of scholarship than illusions are. And many books written about the USSR by disillusioned Communists, Trotskyites, or simply opponents of Communism have shown no finer perception of the reality of Soviet politics than those who exhibited what they thought was sympathetic understanding of the attempt to build a new and better society. One might mention in this connection the fairly universal underestimate both before and right after the war of the USSR's economic potentialities. The same moralizing strain which would not grant a despotism the capacity to industrialize and modernize rapidly may be responsible today for serious distortions of Russia's recent history. We do not require much in the way of corroborative evidence from Khrushchev to realize that Stalin was a sadist and tyrant. But we ought not to accept uncritically the more recent Soviet allegations that he was incompetent and ineffectual as well. Before we swallow the tale of Stalin following World War II's battles on a globe, we might well reread the passages in Churchill's and De Gaulle's memoirs in which the old despot is portrayed as a brilliant and intransigent negotiator with a detailed knowledge of the realities of the world situation. And it is equally well to remember that, before Stalin was able to rule through terror, he had risen to supreme power not only through administrative intrigues but also because of a brilliant understanding of the politics of the Communist Party of Russia in the twenties. Stalin's "campaign" for power within a totalitarian party set a model which in many ways was followed by Nikita Khrushchev in his ascent to supremacy.

The preceding comments are intended to urge a degree of caution upon the writer on Soviet politics and a degree of wariness upon the reader confronted by new "revelations" about the Soviet Union. The years since the war have marked a great improvement in the level of scholarly discussion of Russia and Communism. But the enormously enhanced public awareness of the importance of these two subjects has been productive of some negative as well as positive phenomena. The prewar commentator, whether he wrote with abhorrence or approval of the Soviet experiment, wrote for a relatively small circle of interested readers. Today this new creature, the Soviet expert, Sovietologist, Kremlinologist, or what have you, writes with perhaps an exaggerated sense of the importance and impact of his words. The American public, while more interested in international affairs, has not grown equally aware of the inevitable uncertainties of international life. It becomes impatient with an expert who is suitably cautious in his conclusions and who sketches alternatives rather than giving clear-cut answers and prophecies. The average American has by now absorbed enough homegrown Freudianism to realize that in discussing, say, the marital difficulties of his neighbors, one cannot, most of the time, point to a single clearly delineated cause and prescribe a simple and guaranteed solution. But this sophistication disappears when we ponder the complications of international life. What is going to be the resolution of the Sino-Soviet difficulties? What would be the effect of another succession crisis in the Soviet Union? And no buts and ifs, if you please.

The result of this public pressure for enlightenment, and of the awareness that the statesmen of Washington and London now look hopefully to the formerly ignored professors to provide answers, has often been destructive of scholarly composure. Some experts write of Soviet affairs as if they were under the table when the Presidium of the Central Committee of the Communist Party was conducting its most secret deliberations. Others will hem and haw in their conclusions, for they would rather sacrifice the claim to prophetic powers than be found wrong on any specific issue. The common-sense fact that there are many things about the decision-making process in the USSR that we do not know and that we must surmise, but making sure that we label conjectures as such, encounters a psychological resistance which alarms the more fainthearted among the experts. This writer once witnessed a discussion between an expert and a nonexpert, in which the latter (it was following the events of June 1957) reproached the former bitterly for his previous underestimate of Khrushchev's power and political guile. With a rare fortitude, the expert replied that his mistake had been shared by people each of whom had surely more expertise in Soviet politics than Isaac Deutscher, Edward Crankshaw, and Harrison Salisbury rolled into one, namely by Molotov, Malenkov, and Kaganovich.

On a more serious level, the current tendency of the scholar to don at times the mantle of the prophet and statesman has also been productive of some mischief. All that a study of Soviet politics can render in present conditions is to enlighten us about the recent trends and developments and to offer some clues about the range of possibilities in the near future. We have all been comforted by what has, for the lack of a better term, been called the liberalization of Soviet internal life since 1953. But does this liberalization necessarily augur well for more peaceful relations between the Soviet Union and the West? The following pages more than once offer testimony of how the increased importance of the people's aspirations and expectations, of how the increased complexity of the internal problems faced by the regime, might draw and in some instances have drawn the leaders of the USSR into more reckless foreign policies than might otherwise have been the case. We consider, and rightly, that the Western world has profited and is likely to continue profiting from the insoluble problems of the Communist bloc. But does this general favorable *tendency* preclude the possibility that in an isolated case the very lack of unified direction of world Communism might lead to an armed clash with the West? The death of Stalin has been credited with the improvement of East-West relations and the more relaxed character of the cold war. Again, as a general statement this is undoubtedly true. But, from what we know of Stalin's temperament and methods, it is quite likely that he would, were he alive today, adopt much more hostile policies toward the Chinese and consequently more friendly ones toward the West than Khrushchev and his colleagues have been willing or able to.

The preceding observations might be thought to be perverse and paradoxical. Yet they imply that the student of Soviet affairs has as his first task to be neither hopeful nor pessimistic, but simply to state the facts and tendencies of Russian politics. It is when he begins to see in certain political trends the inevitabilities of the future, and when he superimposes upon them his own conclusions about the desirable policies of America toward the USSR, that he is courting trouble both as a scholar and as a would-be statesman. To be sure, to require complete detachment is to offer in this case a counsel of perfection seldom if ever completely attainable. We all write not only as students of Soviet affairs but also as people desirous of a peaceful future and of the survival and augmentation of democratic institutions throughout the world. But these aims are also best served if the scholar eschews the pose of a prophet and does not confuse his function with that of a policy maker.

I   THE HISTORICAL ROLE OF MARXISM AND THE SOVIET SYSTEM

No analyst of Soviet Communism has failed to express surprise that a Marxist movement should have triumphed in a prevailingly agrarian society. Equally trite has been the observation that the Russian Marxists have not been able to solve the problem of the peasant and his full integration into their socialist system. Marx was a city boy, we are told, and that is why Nikita Khrushchev, the First Secretary of the Communist Party of the Soviet Union, has to spend his time discussing the failure of agriculture to keep up with the industrial sector of the economy. We are left with a truly confusing picture. Marxism, on its own premises designed as a movement for fully industrialized societies, comes to power or is a serious contender for power in societies that are mainly agrarian, while mature industrial countries adhere perversely to something (but something that is definitely non-Marxist) variously described as "the social-welfare state," "liberal capitalism," and the like. Perhaps Marx was wrong and—for reasons unforeseen by him—his system is peculiarly suitable to what we now term backward countries, with predominantly agrarian economies

SOURCE: First published in *World Politics,* October 1955.

and low standards of living. Then why cannot Marxism solve its central problem of agriculture? Or is it perhaps merely one form of Marxism—Soviet Communism—which is thus incapacitated? No wonder that scholars, first secretaries, and the rest of us tend to become confused.

The answer may lie in a paradox: it is the peasant, in the Eastern European sense of the word (which may be similar to the Asian or African one), that is, untransformed into the farmer or the agricultural worker, who makes Marxism relevant as a social force. No peasant—no Marxism. The latter may still exist as a sect or an imposed system of values, but it has no relevance to the social problem. Behind the paradox lies an involved story which has as its major components the Industrial Revolution, anarchism, and Karl Marx.

I

Our textbooks agree that sometime between 1750 and 1850 a major economic and social transformation took place in Western Europe. Favored, especially in England, by the political and intellectual climate of the period and by the advances of science, industry and commerce triumphed over agriculture. The Industrial Revolution, we are further told, involved considerable social and economic dislocation and consequent human unhappiness, but in the end it demonstrated both its inevitability and its superiority as a producer of wealth. Industrialism has become the dominant economic force of modern times. Its meaning is quite simple: an industrialized society has a large number of factories, an extensive network of railways and roads, a well-developed banking system. By the same token, a "backward" country—say, Germany of 1860, Russia of 1880, or China of 1950—in order to industrialize, has to build roads and factories. The technique is well known and the main prerequisites and conditioning factors are capital and natural resources.

But the task of industrialization does not lie exclusively or even mainly in material achievement. A society must be ready to accept it. And, having accepted it, the society must develop a technique for absorbing the shock of new habits of action and thought and new economic forces. In 1857, soldiers of the Bengal army refused to use newly issued cartridges that were reputedly greased with cow's fat and thereby precipitated the Indian Mutiny. Only a comparatively few years ago, the attempt of the government of the Gold Coast to arrest a plant disease by forcing the peasants to extirpate diseased cocoa shoots led to riots. Such examples can be multiplied and they are found not only in colonial or backward areas. Opposition to vaccination and rioting because of the introduction of a new calendar have occurred in quite civilized communities. We cannot simply dismiss such incidents as manifestations of backwardness or religious superstition. They are an overly dramatic and violent expression of the usually more passive hostility with which a nonindustrial society encounters the preliminaries of industrialism: government regulation and science. Progress and education may ride roughshod over uncivilized protests, but, instead of disappearing, the shock of industrialization will become greater even though the reaction to it becomes more indirect and subtle.

The tsarist bureaucrat who opposed railways because they enabled people to travel and acquire disturbing ideas, and his fictitious colleague who wanted to "undiscover" America, are well-known figures in official Soviet humor, which is unaware that a paraphrase of the joke might well be applied to the contemporary Soviet bureaucrat. But the attitude expresses the hopeless wisdom of conservatism: nothing can ever be the same after industrialism has transformed the face of the country and after the people have heard about strange lands with still stranger political and social institutions. We know what the statesmen and theorists thought about the great change: English liberalism adapted itself to the industrial age; the Saint-Simonians built their fantastic, but in many ways prophetic, dreams; Herzen did not like what he saw of the not yet industrialized but already materialistically minded West. What we know less well are the feelings and reactions of the main figure in the industrialization process: the peasant or small craftsman transformed into a worker and thrown into the vortex of the Industrial Revolution. It is assumed that he loses his peasant associations (although we know that in Russia, for a long time at least, the dividing line was not very clear) and his peasant outlook, and that in the second and third generation he becomes a bona fide proletarian.

Yet the transformation has not always been so simple or abrupt. For one thing, at various periods up through the NEP in the 1920s, the Russian peasant often oscillated between the factory and his village rather than definitely becoming a proletarian. For another, any peasant who became a part of urban civilization was not immediately remade into another class personality. Certainly, the values and reactions of the peasant community were not entirely lost; they became a part, and an important part, of the fund of influences which was to shape the outlook of the class being created by the Industrial Revolution. It is a bold man who would attempt to define the precise character of the social inheritance left by an agrarian society to its industrial successor, and bolder still who would try to define the elements of similarity in an English tenant farmer of the eighteenth century, the French peasant who received land during the French Revolution, and the freshly emancipated Russian peasant still confined in the mir. Leaving the task to an economic historian, we may assert that some similarities are visible even to a nonscientific social scientist.

In a preindustrial age, an agrarian community is built around land tenure. Land is property, however much the latter concept may be attenuated by the tenant, serf, or member of a commune. The status that the peasant acquires from the mode and quantity of his property is much more important than any other aspect of his personality. In his daily activities, he does not encounter the institution known as the state. He does encounter authority, which, when it does not emanate from the peasant community itself, emanates from a different kind of social being called the justice of the peace, the landowner, or the district officer. The essence of the authority insofar as the peasant is concerned consists in the unbridgeable gap between the ruler and the ruled and, insofar as the societies in which we are particularly interested are concerned, in the entirely different economic and social status of the ruler, who often combines a proprietary relationship with the peasant with a direct administrative function. The authority is then, by definition, an imposed one, yet *ideally* it is both distant and external and should not interfere with the personal world of the peasant: his religion, his family, and his own "property" and economic function. Since nothing is ideal, there are moments of stress and even rebellion, occasioned by unduly harsh exactions on the part of the authority, by economic distress, or by national and religious grievances. But, statistically speaking, a preindustrial society will give a deceptive picture of placidity and harmony, for the natural radicalism of the peasant, the product of his economic and legal helplessness, is held in check by his natural conservatism: his attachment to a way of life based on the element of property in his status. "Natural" is the key word, for even before the first factory is built in a given country, the workings of industrialism hundreds or thousands of miles away introduce "unnatural" economic and social forces, disturbing what the conservatives considered bucolic agrarian society and what Marx called the "idiocy of rural life."

The next step is more fundamental—industrialism hits with full and direct force. In some countries, the way is prepared by the existence of a well-developed commercial middle class and by a rural economy already enmeshed with a quasi-capitalist mode of production. Elsewhere, it may start under more primitive social conditions. Everywhere, its influence is a disturbing one. Repercussions of industrialism reach into every sphere of social life. Its major symptom is enormously increased labor migration, both seasonal and permanent in character. As to labor migration and its connection with industrialism, a British historian has written rather complacently:

It is hard for one born in a mature industrial region, inhabited by a *race of patient and disciplined factory workers,* to realize the difficulties involved in the deliberate formation of a factory community, even where industrial habits and traditions are already well established among the local population. *In the course of a generation or two* it becomes quite "natural" for people to work together by hundreds in hot, humid, barrack-like buildings for a fixed number of hours each day, regulating their exertions constantly by the movement of tremendously powerful machinery. After a great war, or any other prolonged dislocation of industry, there may be some temporary restlessness among the "hands"; but the routine soon re-establishes itself as part of the ordinary discipline of life.[1]

The language is blissfully Victorian for a book published in the year of the General Strike, but at least the statement indicates that for "a generation or two" a displaced peasant or craftsman will not fit easily into the discipline of a factory. It is the manner and consequences of his "fitting" which are the subject of this essay.

Labor migration produced complete confusion in the values of the peasant, who before the onset of intensive industrialization had already been beset by the mysterious economic and social forces invading his village. Materially, he might gain by becoming a worker; certainly the landless pauper would. But even so, in most cases, he would consider himself *déclassé.* In addition, the new world of factories and towns was full of phenomena which clashed directly with his peasant or craftsman instincts: "the absorption of the displaced workers into other occupations seemed to contemporary observers to be protracted by a prejudice against mill life. It was said that the weavers were willing to starve rather than submit to factory discipline." [2] Yet obviously they would not starve, at least not in the literal sense of the word; they would accept some employment. The worker found himself without the few points of stability of his previous existence.

The discipline and monotony of factory life replace what the sociologists now call the "sense of belonging" inherent in a peasant community. Authority that previously was simply structured and comprehensible now becomes a confusing tangle of parish and town regulations, parliamentary statutes, and the authority of the factory owner and the constable. Its scope and immediacy are now much greater, for even "unregulated industrialism" reposes on a mass of regulations, whether they are internal factory regulations or city and state laws. Human nature would not be human nature if a low standard of living, combined with a bewildering loss of values, did not lead to resentment. The sum of human resentments of an industrializing society is directed, first of all, against the symbol of change, the machine which enslaves people, the owner of the factory, and the new confusing social order in which the state evidently supports the industrialists and landowners. Is it possible that these resentments will disappear without a trace in the course of one or two generations?

II

It is a part of my argument that certain generalizations may be made about industrialization and the reaction to it which are valid not only for the Industrial Revolution of 1800–1850 in Western Europe, but for any society at any time. But the Industrial Revolution, being the first of its kind, offers us the best opportunity to study the reaction to industrialism in its most extensive form (but not the most typical, since industrialism often comes to societies much less well prepared for it). Unfortunately, even here the picture of the impact of industrialism is like the proverbial iceberg: a small part of it visible in the form of theories, statistics, and political and social movements, but the greater part of it, the feelings and thoughts of the people affected by the process of industrialization, submerged. We are forced to speculate about the latter from an analysis of the former. And one of the first and most striking things about industrialism is the volume and intensity of protest that it evokes. Nobody, for example, liked the situation in the industrial England of 1850. The landowner saw his political power diminishing; the aesthete—or any sensitive person—detested the squalor and injustice of industrial life; the worker began to define his grievances as exploitation and the denial of political rights. And even the liberal capitalist or entrepreneur began to suspect that behind laissez faire lurked the civil servant and factory inspector. The second and even more striking thing is that the process continues in a way entirely satisfactory to nobody. We may forgive the economic determinist for being impressed by the fact.

Obviously, society had to find a way of adjusting itself to the facts of industrialism. Industrialism could not have gone on if the upper classes had clung to the ideas of Lord Eldon, if the worker had remained possessed by the instinct which made him engage in the Luddite riots, or if Adam Smith's notions—devised for a commercial rather than an industrial age—had continued to be the sole ideology of the middle class. Part of the adaptation came in the form of liberalism, as it emerged from the writings of Bentham, Ricardo, James Mill, and others, and the speeches of Bright and Cobden. It became the ruling philosophy in England and a powerful philosophy in France, the Low Countries, and elsewhere. Liberalism in England was strong enough to destroy the old type of conservatism and to convert a part of the working class, but essentially it remained the way of adaptation of the middle class. For the worker, the problem of adaptation became, first of all, the problem of self-defense. The first trade unions were designed to meet the most primitive "social security" needs of the worker and to reassure him through their ceremonial and associations that he had a place in society. From what has been said, we would expect, however, that the reaction of the workers would reflect in some way their own physical transition from one type of society to another, from the peasantry and related occupations to the proletariat. Hence we must look to the early labor movements and the work of the early theorists of social protest for signs of this transition.

The movement which fulfills our requirements is anarchism. The definition of anarchism used here is very broad, so broad that it will be objected that a majority of the early socialist movements are arbitrarily tossed into the anarchosyndicalist camp. But we are principally concerned with anarchism as a feeling underlying the various forms of social protest during the Industrial Revolution. As such, its characteristics are easily discernible. First, opposition to centralized political authority—in essence, to the state—and a predisposition in favor of small communities, with the coercive, regulating element of political power reduced to a minimum or, still more fantastic, entirely abolished. Second, an incomprehension of, or outright hostility to, industrialism as a way of living. Division of labor, the barest prerequisite of any modern—not to say, highly industrialized—society, is itself questioned or admitted only as a temporary evil. Anarchism regarded industrialism as something nasty and antisocial, even when it coped with the problem of assimilating it into its theory: the factory, the money system, and its other paraphernalia strip the individual of his social and moral instincts. Third, when introduced into the immediate context of industrial life, anarchism flares up with the genuine flame of class feeling—syndicalism. It preaches a relentless class war which will not allow any partial concessions, and it advocates a variety of devices, from sabotage to the strike, whose systematic and widespread use would bring the industrial life of any country to an end.

The above description may seem confusing if anarchism is thought of as a kind of socialism which dislikes the state and advocates violence, or as something peculiar to the labor movements of the Latin countries. But even if we disagree on a definition of the term, it must be evident that the emotions and principles described above characterized with varying intensity the thought of people like Fourier, Proudhon, Herzen, Hodgskin, and Bakunin, to name a few, and, more important, that they infused much of the ideology and activity of working-class organizations of nineteenth-century Europe. Anarchism, in the sense in which the term is used here, is the legacy of an agrarian society to its industrial successor. It embodies the clash of peasant values with the reality of industrial life. Just as to the conservative industrialism represents the loss of social stability and old values, so to the peasant-worker it demonstrates and accentuates the latent class struggle of the countryside and endows it with political significance.

It is hardly to be expected that anarchism can become a dominant political force on its own. The ideas of Fourier or even Proudhon, when spelled out, cannot form the basis of the social organization of a modern society. Anarchist feeling is too formless, too divorced from the dynamic of economic development, to create objective conditions and organizations capable of absorbing the economic facts of life. Even such practical offshoots of anarchist feeling as the trade unions and cooperative producers' societies become meaningful and functioning economic institutions only after they have lost their peasant and craftsman roots and are impregnated with the values of industrial society. Otherwise, the culmination of anarchism

is the moralistic dream of a Kropotkin or the mystique of proletarian violence and of the General Strike.

Nonetheless, anarchism is a crucial phenomenon of the
industrial age. It is both a symptom and a cause of the imperfect adjustment of society to its developing economic structure. Should anarchism be widespread, it will punctuate
society's industrialization process with a series of political and
social upheavals. And so long as it remains in the interstices of
the social system, a given country will not fully acquire the
ethos of industrialism and the accompanying social and political conditions.

There is no mystery as to what this ethos is. It is the acceptance of the state and the machine. Or, to be vulgar rather than
Hegelian, it postulates the citizen who sees the painful necessity of paying taxes and whose social perspectives are determined more by the quantity of goods and services he can
command than by those related but more intangible categories
called "property," "class," and the "sense of belonging." Just as
in its progress industrialism has to wrestle with this peasant-
originated disease of anarchism, so it develops its own anti-
bodies: the dynamics of material improvement, democratic
institutions, and social reforms. In a few countries, its pace is
so swift that anarchism withers away, leaving behind such
distant and unrecognizable descendants as trade unionism and
cooperatives. The peasant has been transformed into the
farmer; the worker has undergone *embourgeoisement*. Elsewhere, the story is more complicated.

III

The classical statement of anarchist feelings is found in, of
all places, the *Communist Manifesto:* "The bourgeoisie, his-
torically, has played a most revolutionary part . . . It has piti-
lessly torn asunder the motley feudal ties that bound man to his
'natural superiors,' and has left no other nexus between man

and man than naked self-interest, than callous 'cash pay-
ment.'"[3] "The bourgeoisie has stripped of its halo every
occupation hitherto honoured."[4] It "has subjected the country
to the rule of the towns."[5]

It is clear that the sense of the above remarks is made more
"Marxist" if for the word "bourgeoisie" we substitute "industrialism" or the "Industrial Revolution." But the latter is also
denounced more directly:

Owing to the extensive use of machinery and to division of labour,
the work of the proletarians has lost all individual character, and,
consequently, all charm for the workman . . . Modern industry has
converted the little workshop of the patriarchal master into the
great factory of the industrial capitalist. Masses of labourers,
crowded into the factory, are organized like soldiers . . . Not only
are they slaves of the bourgeois class, and of the bourgeois state;
they are daily and hourly enslaved by the machine, by the over-
looker, and, above all, by the individual bourgeois manufacturer
himself. The more openly this despotism proclaims gain to be its
end and aim, the more petty, the more hateful and the more em-
bittering it is.[6]

It is superfluous to underline the essentially anarchist character of this protest. The main enemy is the machine which
enslaves man to the monotony of division of labor and creates
the oppression of the centralized state. The bourgeoisie, with
its hateful and mean ideology of gain (read "liberalism"), is
the class enemy whom the proletariat must overcome, for it is
the bourgeoisie which, through industrialism, has destroyed
private property and therefore the status of the vast majority
of the population.[7] Class war, violence, and revolution are the
only choice for the statusless proletarian whom the Industrial
Revolution has stripped of country and family.

Although the anarchist character of the premises of the
Manifesto has not been widely noticed (many commentators
have been misled by the violence of Marx's attack on the
anarchist-socialists, whom he classifies as bourgeois and utopian

socialists), it is usually recognized that the ultimate aim of Marx is anarchism pure and simple. The state withers away. With it disappear the classes and the division of labor. Here, then, is the "mutualist" and egalitarian heaven on earth already anticipated by Proudhon and Fourier.

If Marxism were only anarchism, it would be lost amidst a multitude of socialist and anarchist movements expressing bitterness and bewilderment at the coming of the Industrial Revolution. If Marxism did not have a strong anarchist element in its make-up, it would have no attraction for the workers in a society undergoing industrialization. It is submitted that the revolutionary appeal of both Hegelianism and Ricardian economics is rather limited. The Marxist system receives its historical significance from its ability to combine anarchism—the most violent protest against industrialism—with an intense cult of technology and a conviction of the historical necessity and blessings of industrialism. The bourgeoisie "has been the first to show what man's activity can bring about. It has accomplished wonders far surpassing Egyptian pyramids, Roman aqueducts, and Gothic cathedrals . . . The bourgeoisie, by the rapid improvement of all instruments of production, by the immensely facilitated means of communication, draws all, even the most barbarian, nations into civilisation." [8] Again, the meaning is sharply defined if we substitute "industrialism" for "bourgeoisie," and the tribute to the revolution is as violent as the execrations against it: "Subjection of nature's forces to man . . . what earlier century had even a presentiment that such productive forces slumbered in the lap of social labour?" [9]

In their youthful work, free of the theoretical vagaries and philosophical murkiness of the later treatises, Marx and Engels displayed incisively the most important, the most operative, aspect of Marxism: it is a technique of adjustment to the facts of industrialism. It expresses all the grievances of the Industrial Revolution and it shows that industrialism is necessary and must be submitted to—and not only from the aspect of the machine. Another abomination, the state, will inevitably become stronger and more centralized before it gives way to the anarchist dream. In the meantime, switching from the role of anarchist to that of social planner, Marx sees his socialist state adding function upon function to its powers: the state is to monopolize banking, transport, and industry. The state (and in the greedy listing of its functions it is almost forgotten that the proletariat is now the state) is to create real industrial armies—especially, Marx says, with a curious presentiment, armies of agricultural workers.

We must now turn to the struggle between anarchism and Marxism which occupied roughly the last thirty years of the nineteenth century. The struggle had been foreshadowed by the clash within the First International between Marx and Bakunin. It is interesting to see how the conflict is interpreted by a contemporary British socialist, who at one point was a Guild Socialist—the closest British socialism ever got to syndicalism:

For Marx, the significant aspect of the contemporary class struggle was the developing consciousness and organization of the industrial workers, and particularly of those who were subject to the conditions of advanced large-scale capitalism. Bakunin, on the other hand, thought of the revolution much more in terms of the instinctive revolt of the most oppressed and downtrodden groups in society—the peasants in the relatively backward areas and the lumpen-proletariat of such cities as Naples, in which industrialism had hardly taken root at all.[10]

Yet, whatever Marx and Bakunin thought, the fact remains that on the battleground seemingly most favorable to anarchism—peasant societies undergoing industrialization, such as France, Italy, and Russia—Marxism managed to fight on equal terms and to prevail as the more important working-class and revolutionary movement, even before the rise of the Soviet Union. Anarchism emerged with the doubtful prize of Spain—the least industrialized among the great European countries. In Germany, there was no contest. In the most industrialized countries of the West, England and the United States, where Marxism should have been the strongest, it fizzled out and anarchism did not compete.

Now, there are undoubtedly several reasons for any particular configuration of social forces and events. Here we are suggesting one of the most obvious: in a peasant society undergoing industrialization, Marxism offers everything in the way of social protest that anarchism does, and more. By embracing it, one does not swim against the current of social development, but with it. In addition, the very antiauthoritarian premise of anarchism renders it organizationally inept, while Marxism, as Lenin was to see, tends to embody the discipline of the factory in its own party structure. By the same token, there is nothing mysterious about the failure of Marxism in a highly industrialized country where the methods and values of industrialism have been assimilated, and where there are no peasants but farmers. It is not the natural moderation of the British and American worker which should be blamed or praised for the failure of Marx in their respective countries. It is simply that both the protest of Marxism (its anarchism) and its lesson (the necessity for industrial and state organization) are largely unnecessary and irrelevant in the conditions of American or British society, whether in prosperity or in depression. When they come to those societies, class feeling and socialism take the form of laborism: economic action to secure a larger proportion of the national income to the working class and political action to ensure economic planning and direction by the state. Both industrialism and the centralized state are implicit in the very postulates of laboristic socialism. In their old age, both Marx and Engels were worried by a specter: the rise and tendencies of trade unionism. Their worries were justified.

Marxism, then, has had little success in becoming the leading revolutionary or working-class philosophy in either the least or the most industrially developed states. It remains to be added that from the point of view of this discussion Denmark and New Zealand, for example, are "highly industrialized" states, because by industrialization we mean social and cultural adjustment. It is admittedly an oversimplification to treat Marxism as a symptom of and a technique for the adjustment of a peasant society undergoing the pains of industrialization, but an oversimplification is not always without its lesson.

Both the value and the limitations of this method are evident when we take up the case of Germany. The Germany from which Marx and Engels emerged was an agrarian society only starting to experience the impact of industrial ideas. Social development in Germany in the nineteenth century cannot be understood if we omit the problem of nationalism and the social and political role played by various religious movements. Yet, even in Germany, the role of Marxism as the assimilator of industrialism is of great importance. Perhaps we shall understand more about German Social Democracy by looking at it in that light than by having recourse to the worn-out categories of evolutionary and revolutionary socialism.

One is struck, first of all, by the fact that Germany's phenomenal industrial growth between 1871 and 1914 was paralleled by an equally rapid and far-reaching growth of the influence and organization of the Social Democratic Party. Just before World War I, it was the most influential, in terms of votes, single political party in the state. It was Marxist, and it enjoyed, to all appearances, the allegiance of the German working class. So far so good: the picture corresponds to the Marxist self-appraisal—a mature industrial society will have a powerful Marxist movement. But, on second thought, the Marxist character of the German Socialist Party becomes a bit suspicious. Its phraseology was Marxist and revolutionary. Between 1891 and 1914, it served as a shining beacon to Marxists all over the world. Yet, in the same period, the German Marxists were incapable of controlling a single important political development in Germany. The successes of German Marxism were of an indirect nature—they constituted the adoption of rudimentary social security *by the state*—and, if our thesis is correct, the very existence and influence of Marxism in Germany were reflected in the successful pace of Germany's industrialization. But, by itself, the revolutionary, powerful German Socialist Party accomplished nothing and, when the Empire embarked on a war, the party meekly followed, thus presaging the capitulation of German labor to Hitler. It is easy to blame everything on Hegel. Here it is possible only to offer a hypothesis. Perhaps by about 1900 the historical mission of Marxism —guidance of the working class to industrialism—had been accomplished insofar as Germany was concerned. The natural evolution of German socialism lay in the direction of laborism, which in German conditions included the struggle for parliamentarianism. That is what Bernstein's revisionism was about. The German Social Democrats rejected revisionism and the party continued to scare the middle class—which now included the peasant—by its revolutionary ideology, while the unrevolutionary reality of the German working class belied the revolutionary program. German liberalism and German socialism thus checkmated each other.

IV

Among other unfortunate consequences, the rise of the Soviet Union has had the effect of confusing the character, role, and influence of Marxism in today's world. The reasons for this confusion are manifold, but perhaps we can throw some light on it by discussing the role of Marxism in the foundation and growth of the Soviet Union. We are returning to the paradox which opened this essay.

There are a variety of interpretations of this problem. To list some of them briefly: (1) The Soviet Union has reached the stage of (Marxian) socialism (Stalin's interpretation). (2) There has not been any true Marxism in Russia since January 1918 (that of an "orthodox" Social Democrat). (3) There *is* Marxism in the Soviet Union, but something has gone wrong with it since about 1925–1926 (various shades of the Trotsky-ites). (4) What has Marxism got to do with the Soviet Union? It is all a struggle for power (some American commentators). (5) Now that Stalin is dead, the mist of totalitarianism may be lifted from Soviet society, and Marxism in its rationalistic and democratic reality may well be fulfilled (some other commentators, including Deutscher in his *Russia: What Next?*).

It is not unfair to say that several of these attitudes are based on the conviction that an ideology is something you look up in a book in order to determine what your policies should be. Thus Marxism has several democratic passages in its literature. Since there is very little that is democratic about the Soviet Union, Marxism can have no relevance to the politics or social development of the country: therefore, it is all propaganda. Or an ideology is relevant only if it is applied under the exact conditions of its formulation, and "The Marxian ideas of the proletarian revolution, the proletarian dictatorship, and the character of a socialist economy were working hypotheses *designed to fit a highly industrialized, civilized, and organized capitalist society with a very strongly developed industrial working class.*" [11] Yet, by the same token, what were the ideas of liberalism, designed to fit an enlightened middle-class society, doing in the still largely agrarian England of the first half of the nineteenth century? An ideology is not only a political and economic blueprint.

Marxism emerged in Russia toward the end of the nineteenth century because Russia was one of the few societies in which its message was relevant. Russia was being rapidly precipitated into industrialism, while her society was of the type which maximized anarchist reaction to industrialization. Marx was never a worse Marxist than when he admitted that the peasant commune—the mir—might provide the bridge over which Russia would pass to socialism, avoiding the stage of capitalism. On this count, not only Lenin and Stalin but also Stolypin showed themselves to be better Marxists. The mir was the fortress of pre- and anti-industrial mentality and organization. The first impact of industrialism, though it seemingly did not touch the life of the vast peasant masses, made the mir the fountainhead of Russian anarchism, with which both capitalism and Marxism had to struggle. Russia, therefore, was the place where there was par excellence an opportunity for a Marxist party which would absorb the elements of protest of anarchism and yet develop a technique for disciplining it. Political repression and other social factors of tsarist Russia did not allow Marxism to exercise its educational role of training the worker in industrialism. Hence the Communist coup d'état of November 1917 (although it was hardly a "state" that was seized at that time) was essentially an anarchist revolution. Achievement of the other part of Marxism—the full industrial revolution—was to take more than twenty years, and in one vital respect this revolution is still not completed.

History does not always award prizes for the correct understanding of historical forces. The success of Marxism as a political movement was based on a series of fortuitous developments, and Bolshevism in particular has been very lucky. But there is an element of superior skill and superior theory in the success of Lenin and his party. It is not exactly a matter of what he said or wanted, for every practicing politician has to have a wide range of promises and postulates. The greatness of Lenin lay in his stateman's gift of perceiving both the theoretical and the practical aspects of every problem. No discussion of theory takes place in a vacuum; every theoretical solution must be applied from an organizational point of view. Insofar as Russia was concerned, Lenin was the only Russian Marxist who broke through Marxian phraseology to the concrete use of Marxism. While proclaiming and believing himself to be an orthodox Marxist, he saw clearly that Marxism was *about* industrialism and anarchism, and that it was more important to see what it was *about* than what it was for. Thus Marx postulated that, as industrialization progresses, the proletariat acquires "gradually and spontaneously" class consciousness and a hostility to capitalism. Using Kautsky, Lenin attempted to show that Marx did not actually mean this. His own view is really revolutionary, insofar as orthodox Marxism is concerned, but, in 1902, already realistic: "The history of all countries shows that the working class, exclusively by its own effort, is able to develop only trade-union consciousness, *i.e.*, it may itself realise the necessity for combining in unions, to fight against the employers and to strive to compel the government to pass necessary labour legislation, etc." [12] The natural tendency of labor movements in many countries is to develop what we call the philosophy of laborism. And Lenin drives this point home again and again. "The economic struggle is the collective struggle of the workers against their employers for better terms *in the sale of their labour power,* for better conditions of life and labour." [13] But Lenin also saw that industrialism sometimes receives an anarchist or syndicalist response as well as a laboristic one. Along with the Economists, or those Russian socialists who would dilute the political in the economic struggle, he arraigns the terrorists, who are the contemporary Social Revolutionaries, the representatives of anarchism on Russian soil: "The Economists and modern terrorists spring from a common root, namely, *subservience to spontaneity* . . . The Economists bow to the spontaneity of the 'pure and simple' labour movement, while the terrorists bow to the spontaneity of the passionate indignation of the intellectuals . . ." [14]

The paradox of industrial development leading the masses

away from rather than toward true socialism was perceived by Lenin as early as 1901–1902. What, then, was the solution for Russia? To create a "substitute" proletariat, a party of professional revolutionaries. The worker would still be its mainstay, for the discipline and habits of factory life make him a good revolutionary soldier when he is enlightened "from outside," but the organization of the party and the flexibility of its program would cause it to resemble an anarchist conspiracy. Bolshevism, then, is an ingenious attempt to preserve the revolutionary cake and eat it, too: to swim with the natural revolutionary forces in Russian society—with the liberal protest against despotism, with anarchy, the workers' attacks against the economic structure, and the minorities' revolt against russification—and at the same time to preserve an ideology openly antagonistic to many of these aspirations. The success of the Bolsheviks had to depend on the assumption that the liberal and the anarchist protests would not become muted, that Russia would not speedily become an industrialized and parliamentary society in the Western sense of the word. The fulfillment *before 1914* of the program for which the Bolsheviks had been fighting would have left them with one of the following alternatives: either to become a small doctrinaire sect like, say, the later Trotskyites or to become a socialist party of the Western type with its Marxism submerged in laborism.

History was decidedly working for the Bolsheviks. There were two major attempts in the early twentieth century to industrialize and therefore to westernize Russia. One was the introduction of rudimentary constitutional institutions after 1905, and the other—in a way, more important—was Stolypin's reforms. Under them, Russia, where industry was growing rapidly, would also become industrialized in spirit. The "separators," the future kulaks, would eventually grow into farmers, while a large part of the superfluous rural population would go into industry. The mir—the real focus of anti-industrialism and hence of revolutionary feeling—would wither away. But the war intervened and the first important consequences of March 1917 were not the dethronement of the Romanovs, but the destruction of parliamentarianism and the partial liquidation of the separators, who in 1917 were forced back into the mir.

Of the two Russian revolutions of 1917, the conventional view has held the March overthrow of the monarchy to have been a "moderate democratic" revolution. Maynard had a better perception of the consequences of March 1917 when he wrote: "In explanation of what happened in rural Russia, let me again emphasize the virtual disappearance—outside of the Mir and the Canton Committee—of all authority. Tolstoi had counselled his countrymen that each should say: 'For me there is no State'. They had taken his advice, and the State had vanished into air, like a castle of dry sand." [15] And not only in rural Russia, but in the cities and the army, the revolution of March 1917 was in effect an anarchical revolution. Few people were killed, and many legal and political institutions seemingly survived. But, in fact, centralized authority disappeared and society became a loose grouping of local authorities calling themselves mirs, soviets, and the like.

When Lenin in April 1917 exclaimed, "All power to the Soviets!" he was expressing something which was only partly an aspiration and very largely a statement of fact. By deepening the anarchist character of the revolution, the Bolsheviks had the best chance of achieving power. Once there, the necessary task of counterrevolution, re-establishing authority, would have to be started.

The history of the first twelve years of the Soviet regime is the history of the interplay of the two contradictory elements of Marxism: the revolutionary (anarchism) and the centralizing (industrialization). The Bolsheviks had been carried to power by a wave of anarchic revolutionary feeling which spread throughout Russia both consciously, in the form of a variety of political movements, and unconsciously, in the general feeling of the country. Their first steps had to manifest a degree of submission to this feeling. It would be too much to suggest that they were hypocritical in their actions. On the contrary, they believed at first that their own revolution was but a prelude to a general European revolution. Hence their acquiescence in the purely revolutionary aspects of their program even if un-Marxist, which at the same time were tactically unavoidable: complete nationalization of industry, which Lenin, looking further than his colleagues, could not have liked, and the grant, however theoretical, of the right of self-determination to the non-Russian nationalities of the Empire and of "land to the peasants." Yet, if concessions were made to what in the broadest sense of the term is, and at times was, actually anarchy, the opposite principle was simultaneously asserting itself. The state—centralized authority—was being re-born in the Central Committee of the Communist Party. The army and the Cheka were the first typical agencies of the state and of a movement which, because it extols anarchy and liberty to such a degree, has need of so much in the way of discipline and centralization. While in his poetry Blok was praising the mystique of anarchism and rebellion against Western civilization, other poets were already extolling the machine.

The civil war over, the Bolsheviks could settle down to the task of constructing a Marxist society. Its essential characteristics begin to emerge even in the midst of revolutionary fervor and mysticism. If Lenin could say, "All power to the Soviets!" in 1917, in 1920 and 1921 he said in effect, "No power to the Soviets!" That anarchism and, consequently, revolution were dying in the Soviet Union was dimly perceived by the instigators of the Kronstadt rebellion, with their plea for "Soviets without the Bolsheviks." If Kamenev, Zinoviev, and Rykov had thought in 1917 and 1918 that it was improper for Marxists to

carry out a coup d'état or to rule without the other revolutionary parties, by 1921 they learned that Marxism at this stage
was neither anarchism nor democracy. Those who did not
learn, the Workers' Opposition, were chastised or expelled
or sent into political exile. The voice of the Workers' Opposition, although it came from the workers and intellectuals, was
the genuine voice of peasant Russia. It pleaded for egalitarianism, decentralization, and local autonomy. To Trotsky, who of
all the Bolsheviks saw most clearly the other side of Marxism,
the syndicalist postulates were to be met by centralization, the
grant of full power to the state, and absorption of the unions.
That he was premature in pleading for these actions there can
be no doubt. It took a dictatorially united party, supported by
an organized machinery of terror, to disarm the peasant and to
destroy the unions in 1929–1930, and even then the struggle
almost wrecked the state. In 1921, the party could not have won
a full-scale war against anarchism and at the same time started
Russia on the way to industrialization. In order to achieve what
Trotsky wanted, Lenin had to compromise on the issue of
unions. But, ironically enough, the struggle had demonstrated
the prevalence of revolutionary and anarchist feelings in the
party itself, and how could it be otherwise? So Lenin had to
sanction the building of a bureaucratic network within the
party, and he had in Stalin a man ideally suited for the task.

How a revolutionary party was transformed into a bureauc-
ratized party, and how Stalin successively eliminated his rivals
—Trotsky, Zinoviev, Bukharin, and others—while ascending to
full dictatorial power, has often been told. But the struggle for
power took place in a Russia where Marxism was the official
ideology but the NEP was the economic reality. The second
installment of Marxism was to come, and how could it do so
with the peasant barring the way to socialism? To a casual
reader of post-World War I Russian history, the obsession of
the Bolshevik leaders with the peasant, the apathetic mass of

peasantry, appears unreasonable, if not morbid. How could Lenin say after the Soviet state had survived the civil war and foreign intervention, "Small-scale production gives birth to capitalism and the bourgeoisie constantly, daily, hourly, with elemental force, and in vast proportions"?[16] Why did the Bolsheviks, in the period under discussion, worry more about the peasant than about "capitalist encirclement"? The answer has already been given. Being Marxists, and we must grant that they were, they were instinctively ill at ease with the peasant. For, quite contrary to Lenin's words, the peasant was *not* a budding capitalist. Under the conditions in Russia in the 1920s, he was an anti-industrial and anti-state force. When the party decided to end the period of retrenchment, the Nepman—the urban petty capitalist—vanished overnight, but the peasant was placed squarely in the way of Marxism.

There were two ways out of the dilemma, and I am here simplifying, in social and political terms, what was economically much more complicated. One solution was to let nature take its course. The kulak was the budding rural capitalist; let him grow into a full-fledged farmer and become the strongest force in the countryside. The less efficient and enterprising peasant could be pushed into the industrial army. The process which had taken place in the West would be repeated in Russia—a Bolshevik version of Stolypin's reforms. This was the process which the Communist Party appeared to encourage in 1924–1925, when the left opposition was scandalized by Bukharin's alleged advice to the peasants ("Get rich") and by Stalin's acquiescence to the peasants' leasing land and hiring help. The real enemy of the party was the person whom every official speaker presented as the natural ally of the Bolsheviks, the "middle peasant" who would not budge one way or the other, who would become neither a proletarian nor a capitalist.

But perseverance in the solution toward which the majority of party members were probably inclined (and it is on this point that Stalin was most persuasive in destroying Trotsky and Zinoviev) would have had a fundamental effect on the character of the Soviet regime; the peasant would become much more of a social and political force. He would in effect determine the pace of Russia's industrialization. And once his *embourgeoisement* had proceeded far enough, would he remain satisfied with economic concessions? The whole framework of totalitarianism built so patiently by Stalin would be endangered.

The alternative solution was adopted in 1927–1928. Both anarchism and the rudimentary capitalism of the countryside were to be done away with. The peasant was to be turned into a worker. Not only the kulaks but the peasants were to be eliminated as a class. "Collectivization" is actually a euphemism for a system which attempts to convert agriculture into a centralized industry. The solution was to be quick and drastic. The Bukharin-Rykov wing of the party, appalled at the actual meaning of collectivization and its consequences, protested briefly and ineffectively. But the peasant resisted, and ultimate victory eluded the regime. By the middle 1930s, the Soviet regime had to give up hope that the outright type of grain factory—the state farm—would become a major element of agriculture. Within the collective itself, the individual had become a major element of agriculture; within it, individual peasants were allowed garden plots and a few other items of noncollectivized property. The kolkhozes today incorporate agricultural workers who have not ceased to be peasants. Like their medieval ancestors, they are *glebae adscripti;* they are workers, but they would like to be farmers. In this triple personality of the Soviet peasant lies the main problem of the Communist government.

V

Beginning with 1930, the role of Marxism in Russia has undergone a profound change. Prior to 1917, and in a more limited sense up until the late 1920s, it was like a sponge, absorbing all that was revolutionary and anarchistic in society. The claims for democracy, for land, for freedom and experimentation in morals and art—Marxism-Bolshevism expressed all of them and many more at one time or another. Having gathered into itself all these forces, Bolshevism proceeded to offer them on the altar of industrialization. It is not the state that withers away; it is Marxism, or its revolutionary and anarchist side. Having destroyed the trade unions as independent organizations, Stalin dismissed as petty-bourgeois nonsense the argument for egalitarianism in wages and for giving the workers a share in management. An exuberant cult of personality and loose morals are notoriously unhelpful to the national economy—something which a Victorian Methodist who was also a manufacturer and a Liberal M.P. had argued a good many years before the Soviet bureaucrats, who made divorce difficult and expensive to obtain and homosexuality a crime. Literature, the newspapers, and the arts should teach useful social lessons rather than being frivolous or disturbing, and so the Soviet writers and artists became socialist Horatio Algers purveying socialist realism. This neo-Victorianism inherent in so many features of Soviet society has been characterized as the "great retreat," and sociologists have discovered social stratification in the society where class conflict had been abolished. Yet it is difficult to view the work of the 1930s as a retreat from Marxism to opportunism. It is the logical completion of Marxism, "revolution fulfilled" rather than "revolution betrayed." Terror and totalitarianism have compressed the decades of industrial revolution in the West into a relatively few years in Soviet Russia. Whatever revolutionary elements were unorthodox and even irrelevant to the main task—industrialization—were destroyed during the great purge of the thirties. Russia, and here we must grant partial justification to the claims of the Communists and Communist sympathizers, proved her status as an industrial state during the Second

World War. Has Marxism in its most totalitarian form shown its superiority as a social and economic technique? Has it really conquered the forces of history and demonstrated that it is the wave of the future for the whole world? Events in Russia since the end of the war offer an answer.

The extent of Russia's industrial recovery and expansion surprised the world. The industrial segment of Soviet Russia has shown amazing strength and dynamism. No longer is Stalin's aim, "to catch up and to outstrip" the West, taken as empty propaganda. Science, the state, industrial discipline—these elements of industrial society are now firmly implanted in Soviet Russia. But Lenin's and Stalin's other challenge, repeated at the beginning of the great transformation in the late 1920s, is still unanswered: "Who will get whom?"—will "they," the bourgeois, anti-industrial, antisocialist forces in Russian society, get us, or will "we" get them? Dialectic has played a strange trick on Soviet society and its rulers. Marxism has destroyed anarchism, or a large part of it, only to give rise to social forces and classes not unlike those against which Marx was raging in the England of the 1860s and 1870s. The Soviet worker has accepted industrialism and, unlike his English brother of the corresponding period, he has been given social security. But, like the industrial worker in any mature industrial economy, he wants the elimination of the speed-up system and output norms; he wants better housing and higher wages: he is, in brief, at the point where the Western worker was ready to discard the syndicalist dream as irrelevant and to plead for real trade unions.

And the new Soviet middle class—the official, whether his place is in the army, party, industry, or labor aristocracy—why should his mentality be essentially different from that of the bourgeois in any advanced industrial country? There is a ready answer: terror and propaganda. But terror will only stifle criticisms; it will not suppress aspirations. Propaganda may indoctrinate insofar as the world outside one's own experience is concerned, but it will not always affect the experience. Acquisition of power and status in the Soviet Union is of course not the same process as in the United States or England, and yet there are considerable similarities. Even the tension of economic speculation at the height of a boom or depression may be very roughly compared to the "political speculation" in which a Soviet bureaucrat or even scientist must engage at times. But we need not push comparisons excessively far. All that is necessary is to observe the system of incentives for the various segments of its middle class which the Soviet regime has either put into effect or on paper: material rewards which make laughable the egalitarian pretensions of the early days of the regime, ranks and orders, and (on paper) judicial security and assorted democratic freedoms. The Soviet middle class wants status and security.

Stalin's original challenge—who will defeat whom, the Bolsheviks or the inert and bourgeois forces in the society?—has thus received a new twist. For at one level "we" and "they" are the same people. One of the most perceptive studies of Soviet society observes on this problem, from the point of view of totalitarian control: "This transformation of the political administrator into a technical one, and the consequent blinding of one of the eyes of the Kremlin, is apparently a matter of great concern to the top Party leadership." [17] But the problem is not primarily one of control. It transcends even totalitarianism and attacks its rationale in Russia: Marxism and the role of the Communist Party and its highest organs as the sole exponent of truth. If Marxism has accomplished its historical mission of bringing Russia from backwardness to the status of an industrial power and one of the two great states of the modern world, what further use have "we" for Marxism? Its precepts sound irrelevant and confusing in the daily reality of Soviet life. And if the fight has been fought and won, can't "we" have a bit less totalitarianism and more security? Why not substitute socialist pragmatism for Marxian doctrine; why not have a kind of bureaucratic *rechtstat* instead of the full vigor of party-driven totalitarianism? If questions such as these were not being asked within the party hierarchy after the war, for whom did Stalin write the following passages: "Some comrades deny the objective nature of scientific laws, in particular the laws of political economy under socialism . . . In view of the special role allotted by history to the Soviet state, they hold, *the Soviet state and its leaders can negate existing laws of political economy, can 'establish' new laws, 'make' new laws*"?[18] And, "The point is that we, as the leading core, are joined each year by thousands of new, young cadres fired with the desire to help us, eager to prove themselves, *but lacking* an adequate Marxist education . . . They are amazed by the colossal achievements of the Soviet regime, their heads are turned by the extraordinary successes of the Soviet system and they begin to imagine that the Soviet regime 'can do anything,' that 'everything is child's play' to it, that it can negate scientific laws and fashion new ones. *What is to be done with these comrades?*" [19] Stalin's intervention on the eve of the Nineteenth Party Congress may be taken as evidence of the dictator's senility, for the questions he asks and the answers he gives must have been heard by the "new comrades" hundreds of times; or it may be taken as a direct warning that pragmatism should not replace Marxism and that the party and its totalitarian controls should not begin to wither away.

The postwar history of Russia may be seen as turning around the definition of the place of Marxism in Russian society. Marxism was kept in the background during the "Patriotic War"; membership in the party became a reward for good service. Once the war was over, nationalism as well as Marxism was used to justify the need for further sacrifices and for continued isolation from the capitalist world. One should not discern world-shaking importance in such petty measures as the introduction of uniforms for some branches of the civil service, the abolition of the title of "Commissar" and the reversion to "Minister," or the omission of "Bolshevik" from the title of the ruling party. Petty and formal as the measures are, however, they are still characteristic. Anything which smells of revolution has become a bit embarrassing to "some comrades." It is curious that no party congress was held immediately after the war to hail the victory. It would be senseless to think that the leaders were afraid of political trouble; it is more likely that they were not sure in what direction to chart the future of the state and the party. The Nineteenth Party Congress of October 1952 looks in retrospect like an attempt to reassert the party's role, and the events of the few months preceding Stalin's death look like a build-up for another major purge. But it is significant that Stalin's death was followed by an amnesty and a laborious demonstration of "Soviet legality" in the release of the Kremlin doctors.

What transcends the personalities involved, the shifts in power, the assassinations and purges, is the basic problem of social forces at work in Soviet society. Omnipotent as it appears to be, the regime still has to deal with social forces as they become translated into figures of production. Marxism has probably industrialized Russia faster than capitalism could have done, but at a far more terrible cost. Marxism has thus done its work, and there must be many who wish that Marxism and the Communist Party in the form they know it would go away. Will the work be undone if Marxism "goes away"? Stalin and the leaders of the Communist Party have thought so, but their opinion is obviously not unbiased. However, an impartial American observer, Barrington Moore, holds with Stalin:

Should the political source of industrial expansion vanish or decline, there is nothing in sight to take its place. From the worker up to the minister, the disappearance of this political pressure would mean the end of that part of his situation which now results in the drive for greater and greater output. Stagnation, as has been indicated at other points, appears built into the structure of the Soviet economy and lies continually just beneath the surface. So far it has not been permitted to develop because of the dynamic leadership at the center. If this factor changes, the entire machine could conceivably grind to a stand-still . . .[20]

I cannot accept Moore's analysis in its entirety. Yet there is one major factor which provides partial justification for it and for Stalin's admonition. Marxism and the party still have tasks ahead in Russia.

We are back with the figure with whom we started: the peasant. If his attitudes and problems had a great deal to do with the rise and original success of Marxism in Russia, his very intractability to Marxism presents the doctrine and the party with a still uncompleted mission. The peasant does not produce enough. Collectivization has subjugated him and has released labor for the factories, but it has not made village peasants into workers. Here then is the current battle of Marxism in Russia, the battle on which turns the future of the Soviet regime.

In Sholokhov's novel on the great collectivization, *Podnyataya tselina,* one of the central characters, a peasant who helped in the collectivization drive, refuses at the end to join the Communist Party. In explanation, he avows that he loyally supports the regime and its objectives, but that a nostalgic feeling grips him whenever he sees the cow he owned pasturing with the collective herd. Collectivization, whether we take the word of a literary propagandist or that of Khrushchev, does not suit the peasant. The problem transcends the economics of production; it goes to the roots of Marxism and Communism in Russia. The only possible types of solution were defined by Stalin. Writing as if of the past, Stalin nevertheless outlined the current dilemma:

The answer is not, of course, provided by the opinion of some pseudo-Marxists . . . They propose to wait until capitalism has

contrived to ruin the millions of small and medium producers, turning them into farm laborers, and has concentrated the agricultural
means of production . . . Obviously Marxists cannot agree to this
"solution" if they do not want to disgrace themselves in the long
run. Likewise unacceptable is the view of other pseudo-Marxists
who would, if you please, seize power and set about expropriating
the small and middle producers in the countryside and socializing
their means of production.[21]

Yet the second course, "senseless and criminal" as Stalin calls
it, was essentially the solution adopted by Stalin himself in
1929–1930 and modified partly since then. The two "pseudo-
Marxist" courses which he outlined are still the only ones open
to the regime, although supposedly a third course, collectivization, has already been adopted. Either the peasant becomes a
farmer—and this can be done by loosening the structure of the
collective farm—or he becomes a worker.

In fact, since about 1931 the Soviet regime has tried both
courses intermittently. Stalin allowed the garden plot, but
talked seductively of the joys of agrarian "communism," when
peasant families would be lodged in apartment buildings and
eat in common dining halls. It does not take much imagination
to see that the great man was obsessed, and rightly so, by the
problem and was pulled this way and that way by his advisers,
especially in his last years. Andreyev proposed a structural
change or emphasis in the kolkhoz, which might conceivably
lead to its eventual transformation into a genuine cooperative,
and in 1950 Andreyev, a member of the Politburo, was severely
reprimanded. Next it was Khrushchev who led in the opposite
direction: he proposed amalgamation of the kolkhozes into
fewer and larger collective farms. Beyond the super-kolkhoz,
he envisaged the agrogorods or agro-cities. But Khrushchev
in turn was repudiated, and in 1951 the idea of agro-cities was
dropped for the time being.[22] With a true Marxist's instinct,
the aging Stalin turned to extravagant technological projects
to solve the social and economic problem. Not only the agro-

city, but far-reaching schemes of canal and forest construction, were to change nature and transform the peasant.

Stalin's death left his successors with the legacy of the unsolved, and in fact insoluble, problem. The issue of consumer goods, the spectacle of factory workers being sent out to construct state farms on the infertile soil of Kazakhstan, are not only indications that Stalin's successors are either courting popularity or quarreling among themselves, but also that social forces are impinging upon both the doctrine and the party. Marxism in Russia is confronted by the industrial state which it has created and which does not need it any more, and by a peasant society which, having provided the rationale for the rise of Marxism, has not proved susceptible to Marxist solutions.

My argument has touched on the role of ideologies and social forces. It would be foolish to interpolate a prediction and assert that the Soviet system *must* become more or less "liberal" in its policies. A totalitarian system does not abdicate of its own free will, even in the face of insuperable ideological or economic difficulties. All that the argument of this essay claims is that, by defining the historical role of Marxism, we see more sharply the current dilemmas of the Soviet system.

2   STALIN AND THE THEORY OF TOTALITARIANISM

Few among the great historical figures have had the good fortune of Stalin. If the USSR continues on its course of internal and external expansion, Stalin's role as a great architect of history will be made secure. Should the system collapse, historians (with the exception of a few carping moralists) will find a lesson in the inability of the successors to continue the work of the great man. It will even be difficult to reconstruct the history of the crucial years, for so much of it has been distorted beyond hope of reconstruction by the official myth-building and by the destruction of records and of men and, one is tempted to add, of events.

A man's historical role cannot be measured only according to his good or bad historical fortune. It is his theory or philosophy of government which helps to establish his historical stature. Stalin was not a political theorist in the proper sense of the word. His theoretical writings consist of heavy, unoriginal, and often tautological arguments designed to deal with the political

SOURCE: First published in *Continuity and Change in Russian and Soviet Thought,* Ernest J. Simmons, ed. (Harvard University Press, Cambridge, Mass., 1955).

problems of the moment. His Marxist enemies may at times forgive him his totalitarian ways, but they are much harder put to forgive what they term his vulgarization of Marxism, his lack of the subtlety and erudition which allegedly shine from the pages of Lenin and Trotsky. But it is clear that from the work, writings, and speeches of the greatest practitioner of totalitarian government there does emanate a theory of totalitarianism. It is not an elegant or original theory, but a most perceptive one in its critique of the weakness of its opponents: liberalism and what there is of liberalism in orthodox social-democratic doctrine.

I

Stalinism is the clear antithesis of liberalism. The world of liberalism, that of a middle-class, intellectually inclined Englishman of the nineteenth century who read Hume and Bentham, was a world of concrete and tangible objects. This frame of reference did not tolerate myths, deities, or even historical forces superior to human volition. Liberalism looked sharply at man's external behavior and refused to look further. Marx and Freud were entirely absent from the *outlook* of liberalism, even though they were more than anticipated by some of its theorists. The view of human nature propounded by liberalism seems, by our current lights, unrealistic; yet, where this unrealistic view is not held by a large number of people, free institutions cannot flourish.

Marxism, in particular, has made the world of liberalism appear unreal. For Marx and Engels, the "competition" and "interests" of liberalism were but surface manifestations of deeper historical forces. Poverty, economic slavery, and political oppression were not just social evils to be overcome by material progress, education, and legislation, but were the unavoidable symptoms of a decaying economic system. What remained of liberalism in Marx and Engels was the rationalistic setting of the new doctrine and its final vision of a world where, after the catastrophes and revolutions, human freedom would be established.

Marxism is both deterministic and revolutionary. The combination was not incongruous in view of the social and economic condition of Europe when Marx and Engels were formulating their theories. It did become bothersome to the faithful toward the end of the nineteenth century. The workers' lot was visibly improving, while capitalism was expanding and consolidating its position. The bourgeois state was beginning to behave in a manner not entirely consistent with its characterization as "the executive committee of the exploiting class." The new situation called for attempts to reinterpret Marxism, and it was one of them which laid the foundations of Bolshevism.

Today the issues which stimulated the revisionists and the Economists in their quarrels with Lenin remain of academic interest, but Lenin's *What Is To Be Done?* is still the most complete expression of the mood which was to crystallize into Bolshevism. Lenin wanted Marxism to be preserved in its entirety as a *doctrine*, but in effect this doctrine was to be interpreted, shifted around, and changed as it fitted the needs of revolution. But Lenin does not advocate the rule of political expediency. On the contrary, *What Is To Be Done?* advocates taking the most difficult road to power, but the one Lenin feels Marx must have meant even though he did not phrase it exactly in Lenin's words.

The shift from Marx's way of thinking is quite obvious. No idea is more violently attacked by Lenin than the idea of the *spontaneous* growth of political consciousness among the workers. Political notions and concepts must come to them from without, not from the circumstances of their economic life and struggle. The notion of the party as a rigidly centralized and controlled body is generated not only by the need to infuse the worker with incontrovertible revolutionary ideas, but also by the general setting and traditions of the Russian revolutionary movement. But what emerges from the very violence of Lenin's language is his genuine totalitarian impulse, which already finds itself awkwardly combined with social-democratic and liberal phraseology. One has to give a push to men, ideas, and events in order to set them on the road to revolution. The definitions of propaganda and agitation are spelled out and through them shines unmistakably the elitist quality of Lenin's thinking. The party which he is about to build is likened to an army with its detachments sent in every direction.

Lenin, as early as 1902, was particularly attracted by the sociological side of Marxism. The worker provides the most suitable human material for revolution because the habits and circumstances of factory work endow him with an instinct for organization and discipline. Bourgeois society creates continually vast areas of ignorance and discontent. It is up to the revolutionary party to transform the apathetic and misdirected discontent of the masses into active and organized revolutionary aspirations. Marxism becomes an analysis of the sociological weaknesses of the bourgeois system. Years later, Lenin took a liberal critique of imperialism by J. A. Hobson and transformed it into a Marxist analysis of the weaknesses of the bourgeois system on the international plane. Internally and externally, capitalism is creating the forces of self-destruction, not only because of its economic development, though that is the master cause, but most immediately through the social and cultural tendencies it generates.[1] Joined with Lenin's theoretical habits was his temper of impatience and intolerance, and he bequeathed it to his party. The Bolshevik Party as it existed prior to April 1917 was a social-democratic party in name and in its own self-estimation, but it was already grounded in the habits of conspiracy and intolerance. It was, in a sense, Lenin's party, dominated by Lenin organizationally and incomparably more so intellectually. The Bolsheviks were hopelessly unsuited to compete for power under peaceful and democratic conditions. They were well prepared to fight for power in the circumstances of social and economic anarchy and political vacuum.

II

Much is made by some writers of Stalin's alleged obscurity and intellectual mediocrity when compared with other leaders of the revolution. Such judgments are usually colored by the conviction that *many* of the old Bolsheviks were endowed with almost superhuman intellectual and oratorical gifts, while Stalin had nothing but a passion for administrative details and work. There were in the early days of the Soviet regime Communist leaders like Trotsky and Zinoviev who possessed the agitator's gift—the gift of inflammatory revolutionary rhetoric. Others, like Bukharin, had a highly developed technique of Marxist scholasticism—the ability to juggle quotations from Marx and Engels and to apply them to any and every concrete situation. It is somewhat naive, and to the persons involved it proved to have been disastrous, to confuse those abilities with intellectual pre-eminence or political influence. Stalin's own appearances at the party congresses and conferences prior to the crystallization of his personal dictatorship denote him as a very effective political speaker. The speeches were clear and precise, not without eloquence and a sense of humor, and they did not reveal, as did those of Trotsky and Bukharin, personal vanity and intellectual arrogance.

Stalin's role in the early postrevolution days and his rise to power have been attributed to his exceptional administrative ability. The main outlines of his political intrigues, of his skillful use of the party apparatus and the control organs of party and state, have all been well discussed. What has not emerged clearly is the reason why the Communist Party, with its strong and discordant leaders, submitted so easily to the iron hand of

Stalin and his apparatus. Where was the original political force which propelled Stalin into such a commanding administrative position?

The answer must be found, first, in the character and historical tendency of the Bolshevik Party even before Lenin's death. It is sometimes asserted that while the Bolsheviks instituted a merciless dictatorship they themselves enjoyed, as long as Lenin was alive and well, a kind of intraparty democracy. The truth is that, after its October victory, the Communist Party began to grope its way toward totalitarianism. Lenin's methods in dealing with his party opponents were different from those of Stalin, but his toleration of opposition was not much greater than that of his successor. To be sure, the veterans of Bolshevism were not yet being publicly humiliated and then imprisoned for disagreeing with Lenin. But they were likely to be censured and transferred to obscure provincial or diplomatic positions. Had a more efficient party machinery been at Lenin's disposal, the penalties would have been much more drastic.

It is difficult, in the last analysis, to have any kind of democracy without democratically inclined people, and the leaders of the Bolsheviks without exception had long before left behind their last lingering democratic ideas. Even while fighting for his political life, Zinoviev was to denounce as an "outrageous libel" the accusation that he wanted to substitute a democratic republic for the dictatorship of the proletariat.[2] While declaiming against the dictatorship of the Secretary General, Kamenev, on another occasion, could submit nothing better as his recipe for governing the party than an omnipotent Politburo, or dictatorship by committee.[3] And as an example of the democratic feeling on the part of another group of leaders, one may quote Rykov's words at the Fifteenth Party Congress, where he declared his full agreement with those who were imprisoning party members for their antiparty (read anti-

Stalin) activities.[4] The quotations are drawn from the post-Lenin period, yet they reflect not unfairly the temper of those who had been Lenin's chief lieutenants.

If the party was already in Lenin's lifetime moving toward a totalitarian pattern, then the only problem was what character and philosophy this totalitarianism was to take. During the crucial years of his struggle for power, Stalin represented himself, and perhaps not entirely hypocritically, as a simple follower of Lenin and a "common man" of Communism leading the party masses in their sorrowful fight against the sinning "leaders." The pose reflected Stalin's understanding of party dynamics. For the party was being officered to an increasing extent, especially at the local level, by young and rather unsophisticated people who had joined it during the war or shortly after the revolution. Such people were different in their habits and thinking from the older revolutionary worker. They were already acquiring the habits and the mentality of bureaucrats. For them, the figure of Lenin dimmed that of any other Communist thinker or leader, and any attack, real or purported, upon the principles of Leninism was a threat to their very existence. It is among this demi-intelligentsia of the Bolshevik Party that Stalinism found its first political base, and the type itself was to become the Stalinist model to be imposed upon the whole of Soviet society.

The struggle for the succession to Lenin took place on several levels. There was still the level of doctrine where Stalin had to assume the unwelcome role of theorist to establish his claim to the only correct interpretation of Marxism-Leninism; there was the level of politics, manipulation, and alliances in the central organs of the party; and there was the field work among the lower party echelons. Every aspect of the struggle was handled with meticulous care, providing an accurate forecast of totalitarian society where absolute political power is supplemented by, but is *not* a substitute for, the doctrinal infallibility of the leader. It is instructive to review some incidents of the struggle, for they provide a necessary insight into the technique of totalitarianism.

The initial fight was against Trotsky. The intensity of the feeling aroused by Stalin against Trotsky and the continuous abuse heaped upon him until and after his assassination is somewhat surprising in view of the fact that Trotsky had, very early in the game, been outmaneuvered and that he never enjoyed great popularity among the party cadres. The choice of the first enemy was dictated not only by political expediency, but also by a correct differentiation between political popularity and political importance. Feared and disliked by the party leaders, without a great following in the party bureaucracy, Trotsky had still enjoyed a unique position in Lenin's entourage. All the others shone with Lenin's reflected glory, while Trotsky's stature was independent and almost as great. He embodied the revolutionary energy and romance of the October Revolution, and it is significant that his main support was found in the Comintern and among the Communist youth.

Stalin's fight against Trotsky was underlined by the difference between two political temperaments both equally totalitarian. One sees problems in their intellectual guise and prepares to attack through oratory and intellectual arguments; the other sees political problems as grounded in habits and organization. Theory and intellectual conviction are necessary, but they come after the main battle has been fought and won. In his political thinking Stalin showed himself to be more militarily minded than the creator of the Red Army. Trotsky counterposed his "world revolution" to Stalin's "socialism in one country" as an intellectual argument designed to give a sense of direction to the Communist regime. Stalin reinterpreted it as a concrete political program, and as such it appeared visionary and ridiculous. What does Trotsky want? asked Stalin in effect at the Fifteenth Party Conference. And

with his now firmly ingrained habit of answering his own
questions, he gave these answers: Trotsky wants the Soviet
regime to postpone the building of socialism until revolution
sweeps the West. He wants the young and weakened Soviet
state to risk its existence in a foolhardy war upon all the
capitalist powers.[5] In addition, added Stalin piously, the opposition wants us to alienate the peasant by exploiting him under
the cover of a war against the kulak. The opposition, which
then consisted of Kamenev and Zinoviev in addition to Trotsky,
was completely dumfounded. Beaten before organizationally,
they now found themselves in an ideological and political
morass from which they could not extricate themselves. Such
theoretical attempts as Trotsky's statement that the building of
socialism in one country could not be finished while capitalism
survived elsewhere would have been regarded at one time as
a fine example of Marxist sophistication and subtlety. The
assembled party functionaries now heard them with grim incomprehension. It was as if Lenin, after proclaiming "all power
to the soviets," were immediately denounced as a counter-
revolutionary and defeatist, since the soviets were not at the
time controlled by the Bolsheviks.

Trotsky's defense had some of the old brilliance with which
he could sway even a hostile audience. In 1926 it was still
thought important to have some classic Marxist oratory to
throw back at the opposition, and Bukharin was delegated to
match Trotsky and Kamenev in the art of quoting Marx and
Engels. Bukharin spoke in most vituperative tones, drawing
Stalin's ungrudging admiration: "Well, Bukharin, well. He does
not speak; he cuts with a knife." [6] But what was to be the
wave of the future was more succinctly expressed by Stalin
when he ventured to say that, were Engels alive at the moment,
he would undoubtedly exclaim: "may the devil take the old
formulas: Long live the victorious revolution in the USSR!" [7]
He was never again to be as blunt in his appraisal of the role

of theory as in the moment of his triumph over the despised theoreticians and intellectuals of the party.

The Fourteenth Congress and the Fifteenth Conference provided the most dramatic moments of the struggle against the Left Opposition, though the real struggle had taken place before and behind the scenes. Kamenev and Zinoviev, in terminating their alliance with Stalin and in trying to combat his political ascendancy, fell into an ideological trap similar to the one provided by Stalin's "socialism in one country." They attacked the policy of concessions to the peasant, seeing in it a challenge to the socialist character of the revolution. Again Stalin could appear as an advocate of revolutionary "normalcy" and common sense. His new allies, Bukharin, Rykov, and Tomsky, really believed in the policy of concessions and in gradual and cautious industrialization. He himself probably took a pragmatic point of view: the policy of full-scale attack upon the peasant ("kulak" is used almost constantly as a euphemism for all peasants) was not indicated at the time (1924–1926), and in any event a decisive social struggle could not be waged before the party had been firmly united under his hand. But to the assembled party Stalin defended the policy of concessions and moderation as an ideological principle. The majority of the party functionaries, some of whom were of peasant origin, could not but respond favorably to the policy of moderation and to the call to eschew violent experiments and repression. It is only after the opposition had been chastised that Stalin was willing to reveal some of his inner thoughts on the subject—the Bolsheviks have not one but three plans for dealing with the peasant problem, and the one they will apply depends on the concrete revolutionary circumstances of the moment.[8] Kamenev and Zinoviev let themselves be maneuvered into a rigid and untenable ideological position.

At the Fourteenth Party Congress Stalin had to withstand a vigorous assault upon his position. His handling of the party, his attitude on foreign affairs, and his economic policy all came under the determined fire of a minority of the congress. Kamenev and Zinoviev, as yet estranged from Trotsky, were leading the solid bloc of Leningrad delegates. Stalin's position was secured by his alliance with the leaders of the future Right Opposition. Yet, in spite of this overwhelming numerical superiority, the dictator took the most meticulous care to meet and refute every accusation. In his introduction he mentions with approval the Soviet leaders' alleged habit of reporting to foreign workers' delegations, denouncing indignantly the mutterings (which, if heard at all, came from his faction) that foreign Communists are a lot of bother and expense.[9] Here, some delegates must have reflected with emotion, was the man accused of being unmindful of the needs of the world Communist movement. Modestly refusing to indulge in personalities, Stalin revealed his willingness to step down as Secretary General when the party leaders wanted to transform the Secretariat into a political organ.[10] His indignation was aroused by the Kamenev-Zinoviev attempt to demolish Bukharin: "We will not give you his blood" [11]—the blood of the leading theorist of the party.

It fell to Stalin's partisans to denounce and ridicule the opposition. But the opposition itself was tied up in its own contradictions and confusions. To replace Stalin's dictatorship, Kamenev could only propose dictatorship by committee—the Politburo. Yet, it was pointed out, the leaders of the opposition were in fact in the commanding state and party position; Kamenev, for instance, presided over the Politburo, and Sokolnikov over the Commissariat of Finance.[12] It was not Stalin's fault if the administrative ineptitude of the oppositionists was so great that all practical policies had to be formulated by Stalin!

The opposition was caught in a dilemma of its own making. If the "interests of the proletariat," that is, the party, were superior to democracy, how could it object to being treated undemocratically by the majority of the party? The time to protest was in 1912 or in October 1917, but, while assailing Stalin's undemocratic chicaneries and manipulations, Kamenev and Zinoviev were fervently apologizing for their democratic scruples before the October coup. The opposition made the point that its numerical weakness at the congress reflected the faulty social composition of the party. Were the party more proletarian, it would, like the workers of Leningrad, follow Zinoviev. But the strength of the opposition in Leningrad reflected not only the agitational skill of Zinoviev, but the same type of machine politics which Stalin was employing more successfully and on a larger scale.

It was in the course of his struggle against Trotsky and the Leningrad opposition that Stalin used the psychological devices that later became his standard techniques of propaganda. Marxist politicians, and among them par excellence the Bolsheviks, have often appealed to something very deep in human nature by their ability to see "hidden significance" in perfectly obvious and self-explanatory events and statements. The Mensheviks and the Social Revolutionaries in fighting the Bolsheviks were not just fighting their political enemies; they were "really" supporting the capitalists and landowners in their counter-revolutionary schemes. In presenting the peasant policy of Stalin and Bukharin as antisocialist, Zinoviev gave the hypothetical case of a Menshevik who wanted to return to Russia supposedly to pursue his antirevolutionary designs. Were he allowed to return, would he openly embrace the kulak's cause? "No, he would accuse us of underestimating the middle peasant." [13]

Conscious of the strange fascination for the semieducated mind of "inside stories" and "plots," Stalin already in 1924–1925 shifted his attack to the general character of the opposition. Was the opposition really what it purported to be, a group within the party fighting for its point of view—or was it something else? The question was asked more and more insistently, and it was not without its point to the people who had spent the days before the revolution in an atmosphere of suspicion, always on the lookout for an agent provocateur. The preliminary admission demanded from the oppositionists, after their defeat and as a price for remaining in the party, was that they should acknowledge their ideology to have been not Bolshevik but social democratic and antirevolutionary. The way of dealing with the opposition—any opposition—was to be indicated by Stalin at the Sixteenth Congress when speaking this time of the Right Opposition: "What does the Congress want from the former leaders of the opposition? Recantation; self-flagellation? Of course not. Never will our Party . . . demand from its members something humiliating." [14] The Congress wanted *only* three things; an admission that the "line" of the oppositionists led to capitalism; a resolute fight against their own views; and that they should fight against the opposition, that is, recant and denounce themselves. Repeated several times throughout the speech is the phrase: "If you don't press these people, you don't get anything." [15]

Another example of the recourse to the reservoir of deep-rooted prejudice and hysteria was the undercover anti-Semitism, which was used freely in the struggle against Trotsky, Kamenev, Zinoviev and their followers, many of them also Jewish. Ostensibly the dictator and his party struggled against anti-Semitism as an ignominy and barbarism. Some of Stalin's most effective henchmen, like Kaganovich and Yaroslavsky, were Jewish. But no weapon was scorned if the task was urgent. While denying the anti-Semitic charge against Stalin's faction, Yaroslavsky quoted several instances of anti-Semitic slander indulged in by local party organizations and directed against Trotsky.[16] Such an appeal to popular passions and prejudices for the resolution of a party conflict would have been unthinkable in Lenin's time. Its use by Stalin marks an important advance in the totalitarian technique. The ideas and formulas of Lenin, still coldly intellectual in their phrasing, are now beginning to be buttressed by frankly irrationalist techniques.

After 1925 the leadership still remained collegiate in its appearance. The new troika, like the Three Musketeers, consisted really of four people. Rykov, Tomsky, and Bukharin were more firmly entrenched in the party than Stalin's former coadjutors had been. They enjoyed genuine popularity, and Tomsky, at least, had the organizational backing of the trade unions. At one point, in the period 1925–1927, Stalin himself appeared to be a captive of Bukharin's evolutionary economic policy. Stalin's crushing victory at the Fourteenth Congress was secured with the help of the future Right Opposition. It was Uglanov who steered the Moscow delegation away from its projected alliance with Leningrad and averted the danger of the two capitals combining in revolt against the regime—a specter too reminiscent of 1917.

The Right's acceptance of Stalin's dictatorship was conditioned upon the character of his policies and his behavior within the party. His dictatorship appeared preferable to that of Trotsky or of the Zinoviev-Kamenev bloc. In retrospect, it is easy to blame the Right for its blindness and to forget that it would not have fared better, at least initially, in the event of Trotsky's or Zinoviev's victory. Its error lay in allowing Stalin to subvert the party's machinery and to set the precedent for the ejection and humiliation of the Bolshevik oligarchy.

The whole complex of causes, political, social, and economic, which led to the real Russian revolution—the collectivization and industrialization of the late twenties—remains still to be fully investigated and understood. The defeat of the Right Opposition and the final clamping of totalitarian shackles upon the whole nation could not have taken place without the feeling of dynamism and mission aroused among the rank and file of the Communist Party. It showed once again how a totalitarian movement needs a concrete and visible enemy as well as a constructive task in order to display its full character and energy. The campaign was against the kulaks—actually against the mass of the peasants. Behind the kulak theme, Stalin's propaganda arrayed a suitable representation of the regime's enemies, real and imaginary, including Trotsky. The campaign for industrialization also had to have its proper demonology. "Wreckers" and disloyal engineers were uncovered to spur the faithful to ever greater watchfulness and production. Left behind like the Chekhovian figures of daydreaming and indecision, to whom Stalin compared them contemptuously at the Sixteenth Congress, were the leaders of the Right Opposition. They themselves had to go through the routine they had helped impose upon Kamenev and Zinoviev and their followers: vilification, public recantation, and demotion.

A novel of collectivization in a Cossack village, Sholokhov's *Podnyataya tselina,* pictures vividly the stereotypes the regime was trying to impose upon the population. The story opens and ends with a counterrevolutionary plot—no matter how great the successes, the class enemy is always somewhere. The official myth does not completely erase the facts: the overzealous and brutal party functionary whose eyes are opened by Stalin's "Dizzy with Success" speech, the frankly lying agitator, and the anguish of the mass of the peasants are portrayed with full realism. The aims and methods of the struggle do not stop at industrialization and collectivization. What is at stake is the creation of a new type of Soviet personality.

III

At the Sixteenth Party Congress, in June 1930, Stalin was hailed as the leader, and he fully accepted the role he had so modestly repudiated at the Fourteenth Congress. The victory within the party was complete; there were no oppositions to be conquered. The struggle was now for the totalitarian transformation of society.

The speeches of the leader begin to assume the character usually associated with Stalin's oratory: they are didactic, increasingly and unbearably repetitious. They are speeches of a pedantic schoolmaster to a crowd of semicivilized pupils. There is no longer the problem of convincing anybody; there remains only the problem of instilling the right ideas and motivations, first in the bureaucracy, then in the population as a whole. The teacher also assumes the role of theorist. He is no longer the bold pragmatist who could exclaim: "To the devil with the old formulas!" The more the reality of everyday life in the Soviet Union departs from Marxism, the more important it is to show every departure to be in accordance with the spirit and letter of Marx and Lenin. At the Seventeenth Party Congress he elucidates his slogan that the collectivized peasant should become prosperous. Is it the same thing as saying that the peasant should become rich, the slogan that Bukharin and other counterrevolutionaries advocated during the NEP? Of course not. Stalin goes into a long, semisemantic, and quasi-dialectic effusion designed to show that being "rich" is anti-revolutionary, while being "prosperous" is in strict accordance with Marxism. Has Marxism anything to do with the tendency toward equality? Does it advocate equalization of wages under socialism? Of course not. Marxism is an enemy of "uravnilovka." Let us not burden socialism with some petty-bourgeois notion of equality.[17]

Having become fully totalitarian after 1934, the regime from now on will eschew easy pragmatism as a substitute for ideology. Every departure from Marxism has to be done in the name of Marxism, and not as a step justified by temporary expediency. Stalin realized that the people would endure a great deal in the name of an ideology but that they would balk at purposeless suffering. Occasionally, then, while building a stratified caste society, the regime will initiate a discussion of the final stage of Communism.

It is important to analyze the regime's attitude toward ideology: totalitarianism cannot be complete without an ideological basis. Fascism and National Socialism, the latter having some ideological pretensions but never taken very seriously by its proponents, foundered upon military adventurism. They both reached the point where the series of military conquests became the only way of perpetuating the regime. Stalin saw more clearly that an elitist society and dictatorship require an ideology if corruption and privilege, and sheer human restlessness under the denial of all freedoms, are to be held in check. Every dictator wants (but seldom obtains) a government of laws and not of men—except insofar as he himself is concerned. Stalin wanted every Soviet citizen to be ideologically motivated, with the proviso that he himself formulate and interpret the ideology.

Terror and ideology became indissolubly linked in the Soviet system. In his famous letter to *Proletarskaya revolyutsiya* in 1931, Stalin attacked all the historians of Bolshevism, including his most slavish apologist, Yaroslavsky, for their failure to present Trotskyism in its proper light.[18] Some Bolsheviks evidently still thought of Trotskyism as having been a deviation *within* the Bolshevik Party. How could they fail to realize that the slightest tinge of liberalism in dealing with that treasonous and counterrevolutionary grouping was in itself anti-Soviet? Stalin's raving tones in the letter, ostensibly caused by some unsensational historical observations of an obscure Soviet publicist, presage the great purge of the thirties. Isaac Deutscher saw the Moscow trials as a result of Stalin's apprehension about the coming war and of his fear lest the former oppositionists turn against him during an invasion and defeat. We do not know the chain of causes which unleashed the terror of the middle and late thirties. It is, however, at least probable that the trials were staged to serve as the final revision of party history. Otherwise the old Bolsheviks could have been liquidated quietly, the fate which befell Rudzutak, Kosior, and others most closely associated with Stalin in his struggle for power. The new state with its new constitution—"the most democratic constitution in the world"—had no further use for the ghosts of the past. The departing opposition could perform one last service: it straightened out the party's history and provided a suitable explanation for the sufferings and shortcomings of the first five-year plans.

The only opposition Stalin was encountering by the late thirties was from the social forces created by the regime itself. The peasant had been only incompletely defeated. The kolkhoz enslaved the peasant, but its very concept underwent a significant modification from the original formulation. In his speech to the agricultural shock workers of February 1933, Stalin, with the jovial vulgarity he assumed on such occasions, reassured the delegates, promised a cow to every peasant woman, and criticized the local officials for their highhanded ways.[19] The peasant with his instinct for private property and his small individual plot had remained on the agenda of Communism.

Elsewhere the regime discovered that the price for a highly industrialized society was the creation of a privileged class of directors, technicians, and shock workers. The same phenomenon then spread to the state and military bureaucracy. Perceptive sociologists have noted how, with industrialization and the new class society, the Soviet Union began to acquire official mores, ethics, and aesthetics that were sometimes more reminiscent of Victorian England than of post-October Russia.

The war gave a startling demonstration of how the new social atmosphere encroached upon the old ideological impulses. Already in the early thirties Stalin had chastised some of the Soviet historians and writers for their, until then official, negative attitude toward Russia's past. Now the appeal to patriotism, and especially Russian patriotism, all but extinguished the ideological motive. Stalin at the end of the war, in his famous toast to the Russian people, spoke with genuine gratitude of the willingness of the people to support the government. He was not, it seems, among the least surprised.

But the war with its victories and territorial expansion, and the postwar era with its prodigious economic recovery and growth, did not diminish the gravity of the main dilemma confronting the regime. The great purge had destroyed the remnants of the Bolshevik Party of the Lenin era, and the purge had to be arrested lest it destroy the Soviet state. Zhdanov's report at the Eighteenth Congress in 1939 abounded in incidents illustrating the utter demoralization of the party through the hysteria and endless denunciations of the purge. The Communists swelled their ranks during the war, but now a party card became simply a badge of success and privilege in any field of activity. No party congress or conference took place between 1939 and 1952. The Central Committee seems to have atrophied. The Politburo became identical in composition with the very top of the state hierarchy. The logic of events pushed the party and its ideological meaning into the background and was transforming the Soviet Union into a purely bureaucratic dictatorship.

To Stalin, and probably to the more thoughtful members of his entourage, the situation must have appeared menacing. Their view of totalitarianism had always implied that there must be in society no class or group capable of developing a viewpoint or an esprit de corps of its own. Various groups and classes might be accorded concessions and privileges, but never security. The rulers had in the past chastized every social class and every element of the state machinery—peasants, workers, the army hierarchy, the secret police. Yet the very system had created a new middle class of bureaucrats and technicians.

They were no longer, as in the earlier period of the revolution, merely "specialists" tolerated by the party. They were now within the party and comprised much of its hierarchy. They were not unlikely to develop, like the other middle classes before them, a thirst for intellectual independence and legal security. It is possible to see in the series of legislative measures dealing with the most outward characteristics of the Soviet Union a policy of appeasement of the new class. The re-emergence of elaborate uniforms, titles, and decorations, the abolition of the title of Commissar, and, finally, the elimination of "Bolshevik" from the title of the ruling party were some of the concessions, whether conscious or not, to the new spirit. They tended to enforce the impression that the old revolutionary romanticism and the old quarrels and purges were a thing of the past.

But just as insistently the regime, then and now, has refused to abandon the really important elements of its totalitarian creed. The campaign against cosmopolitanism, for all its nationalistic undertones, was designed to destroy any possibility of an independently thinking and writing intelligentsia. While still clearing away some obsolete relics of Marxism, as in the field of linguistics, the regime was also trying to revive revolutionary dynamics and to attack the status quo in agriculture.

There is no reliable evidence as to the significance of the disturbances which affected the Soviet regime before and after Stalin's death and as to the meaning of the "doctors' plot." Stalin's personal dictatorship must have assumed a different character after the war, when in view of his advanced age he no longer could have exercised simultaneous and detailed control of the most important departments of the state and the party. But it is probable that the Nineteenth Party Congress reflected the conviction of the regime that the process of bureaucratic consolidation had gone far enough and that Soviet society must be given another reorientation if bureaucratic ossification were to be avoided.

Stalin's *Economic Problems of Socialism*,[20] his "ideological" testament as it turned out to be, reflected the same motif: the need of totalitarianism to persuade its elite that there is "something else" in the art of government in addition to the performance of concrete political and economic tasks—and in addition to the enjoyment of privileges. The attempt is pathetic in its theoretical incoherence and its pleading insistence that there must be some laws to guide the state and society. It is at once a theoretical defense of the kind of society arrived at in the USSR and a plea not to be fully satisfied with it. The essay states its political aim when it pictures the new cadres joining the party as having been brought up in the spirit of uncritical pragmatism: "What to do with these comrades? How to educate them in the spirit of Marxism-Leninism?" [21] This question Stalin fails to answer, for his real aim is not to formulate a doctrine or to reinterpret one, but to endow the new ruling class with a frame of mind which was peculiar to himself and to his generation.

It is still too early to draw any lesson from Stalin's experiments in social and psychological engineering. The condemnations of Stalin serve the political ends of the present rulers of Russia, but do not change the fact that their methods are still, with some modifications, Stalin's. It must be suspected that the concept of human nature toward which totalitarianism strives is as much of a myth as the early liberal ideas: the apolitical man who responds obediently to artificially stimulated hysteria and indoctrination and who seeks only security and rewards has not been perfected in the Soviet Union. Some writers have seen in Stalin, to quote a famous parody on historical writing, "a bad man but a good thing," a tyrant who created the necessary material prerequisites for a future democracy. Such judgments are based on some very shallow historical comparisons.

The Bolsheviks took over not a barbarous country but a rapidly industrializing and developing society. Stalin, while not entirely successful in his totalitarian aims, destroyed completely and beyond the possibility of an early restoration what there was in the way of humane and democratic forces both in Russian Marxism and in Russian society.

3 SOVIET IDEOLOGY AND SOVIET FOREIGN POLICY

None of the perplexing problems of contemporary international affairs has given rise to more confusing discussion than the relationship of Soviet ideology to the foreign policy of the USSR. The very vagueness of the term "Soviet ideology," or "Communist ideology" (and are they synonymous?), the uncertainty to what extent this uncertain force motivates the makers of Soviet policies, have compounded our difficulties in understanding the behavior of one of the world's two great powers. Are Russia's rulers motivated by cynical power politics? Are they ideological fanatics? Is the content of their ideology the gospel of Marx, Engels, and Lenin, or something else? Questions can be compounded ad infinitum.

This is no academic problem, for the West has sought some way of understanding the basis of Soviet policies, some means of both peaceful accommodation with the USSR and preservation of the confines of the free world. The means hinge on the character of Soviet policy. John Foster Dulles formulated one approach to the problem, viewing Soviet ideology as

Source: First published in *World Politics*, January 1959.

exerting an influence on the foreign policy of the USSR. Proclaiming the peaceful content of democratic ideology, Dulles wrote: "Unhappily, it is otherwise with the creed of Communism, or at least that variety of Communism which is espoused by the Soviet Communist Party." Marx, Lenin, and Stalin have all consistently taught the use of force and violence and Dulles saw the relationship between ideology and action as a fairly direct one, for he went on to say, "These teachings of Marx, Lenin and Stalin have never been disavowed by the Soviet Communist Party of which Mr. Khrushchev is now the First Secretary . . . Therefore, I believe that it is necessary that at least that part of the Soviet Communist creed should be abandoned." [1] And the dependence of the international behavior of the USSR on its alleged philosophy is also maintained by those who, unlike Dulles, believe that the ideology does not necessarily encourage the use of force or violence. A British political scientist sees the content of the Bolsheviks' ideology as a reassuring rather than a depressing portent for world peace. "They will, while they retain their present philosophy, understand neither our society nor their own . . . We cannot rely on their good will, but we can, if we act wisely, rely on their patience. Their false philosophy teaches them that time is their ally; and the more they can be persuaded to let time pass quietly the better for us and for them. Let us at least thank God that Hitler is dead and that the dictators we have to deal with are sane." [2]

The crucial problem is the meaning of the term "ideology." Most of us if asked about the meaning and content of our own ideology would begin by recognizing that, while in many cases it is the product of certain ethical, religious, and political teachings, the relationship is never simple, but modified by a large number of factors: the conditions of our material and social life, our experience, and so on. We do not usually assume that the motives and aims of the policies of the United

States or Great Britain can be fully explained by the ideas of John Locke, Thomas Jefferson, or John Stuart Mill. "Freedom," said a famous English jurist, "has been secreted in the interstices of procedure." And, to paraphrase, the Western notions of freedom, of the proper aims of politics, foreign policy included, have been formulated through the experience of life, the experience of trying to realize the precepts of democracy and liberalism. The more sophisticated writers on the Soviet Union and Communism have realized that one cannot explain the behavior of the rulers of Russia, or certain aspects of the spirit of Soviet society, by pointing to a passage in the *Communist Manifesto* or a phrase from Stalin or Lenin. But in our search for the meaning of Soviet ideology we have not fully recognized that that ideology has been secreted in the interstices of the totalitarian system, which has now existed for over forty years, and that the early millenarian Communist faith has been modified by the experience of almost two generations' application of the original theories to the stubborn facts of life.

We should not, however, go to the other extreme and assume that the rulers of Russia have remained totally unaffected by the doctrines in which they have been brought up and which they have been proclaiming. The relationship between ideology and action eludes a straightforward definition, but it is naive to assume that a group of men, even when endowed with totalitarian powers and with what to an outsider appears an infinite possibility of political manipulation, can remain unaffected by their habits of thought and speech and can indulge in unrestrained Machiavellian politics. At times, tired of explaining Soviet politics by quoting from the scriptures of Marxism-Leninism, we assign the role of ideology to the realm of "propaganda" with which the leaders of the Communist Party of the USSR beguile their subjects while they themselves enjoy cynical freedom from ideological scruples. But, again, the picture is not so simple. Khrushchev and his colleagues may think primarily of expanding their power and increasing that of the USSR, but their choice of means to that end is inextricably intertwined with their philosophy of power, in which ideology plays a crucial part.

The content of what must be called the working creed of the Soviet leaders is not easy to define. It is not wise to seek a definition which ignores the changing character of Soviet society and the changing generations and personalities of the leaders. But it is possible to make certain generalizations and then to see how they apply in the Soviet evaluation of the outside world.

I

The original doctrine of Marx-Engels still remains the official creed of the Soviet Union, but somewhat in the manner in which a modern secularized society acknowledges that it is based on religion. Gone in Soviet Russia today is the sense of the practical immediacy of the socialist doctrine which characterized the ten or fifteen years after the November Revolution. The reasons are manifold. One of them may be that Marxian socialism, as interpreted first by Lenin and then by Stalin (and I shall not enter here into the question of whether this is the "correct" interpretation of Marxism), has as its two main historical functions, first, the channeling of the revolutionary impulses of a society undergoing industrialization and, second, the guidance of this society toward the achievement of a modern industrial state.[3] If this is essentially correct, then Marxian phrases and prescriptions simply have very little immediate relevance to the problems of the Soviet state and society of today. Paradoxically, the success of Marxism in Russia has meant its decline in importance, insofar as the original doctrine of Marx and Engels is concerned. If this statement appears extravagant, let us look at some concrete examples. Is the average citizen of Russia, or a Soviet leader when not giving an official speech, really concerned with the problem of creating an egalitarian society? Is the world revolution viewed with the same intensity of feeling or related to the internal problems of the Soviet Union as it was in the first few years after the revolution? It is unlikely that a member of the Presidium loses any sleep over the meaning of Marxian "negation of negation" or over any other subtleties of the dialectic which once constituted the intellectual fare of the Communists and, what is more important, which were bound up with the actual problems of the internal and external politics of the USSR. Phrases from Marx and Engels will still take their place in official speeches, and in the philosophical journals obscure party hacks will adorn with scriptural invocations the latest economic or political decisions of the government. And the doctrine will be stretched to justify any practical needs of policy. Collaboration with the West was not only the logical outcome of the dire need in which the Soviet Union found itself after the German attack, but was also a theoretically correct application of the Marxian injunction to collaborate with the progressive part of the capitalist camp against its reactionary component. The possibility of peaceful coexistence and the unavoidability of a clash "sometime" between the camps of socialism and capitalism are interchangeable ideological interpretations given out with equal facility according to the turn of international events.

What then remains of original Marxism that is pertinent to the actual conduct of Soviet policy as distinguished from the language in which this policy is proclaimed or rationalized? First of all, there is no doubt that the tone of Soviet policies, domestic as well as foreign, is still greatly affected by the original Weltanschauung of Marx. The father of modern socialism proclaimed his theory at a time when the tendency of liberalism was to proclaim the eventual solution of international difficulties and the harmonious coexistence of nations. *Without*

necessarily assimilating all governments to the same pattern,
free trade, the liberals believed (and the term at its broadest
meant a free interchange of people and ideas as well as goods),
would bring about a degree of international harmony, with
such irrational phenomena as war and imperialism gradually
withering away. The general tenor of Marx's philosophy was
to discount the notion of an automatic harmony of interests
within an industrial society and, by the same token, in international relations. He held that in the world at large, just as
within an individual society, growth, development, and clashes
of interests and struggles were unavoidable and would continue until socialism became the predominant, if not the only,
form of social and political organization.

This legacy of Marxism has become an important part of the
Russians' habitual view of international relations. It has expressed itself in two general characteristics of Soviet foreign
policy. The first has been an unusual sensitivity to economic
and social developments in states playing a major role in international relations. The United States or France, for instance,
does not appear in Soviet eyes primarily as a state having
certain historical and power interests qua state, but as a con-
glomeration of class interests and certain social and economic
pressures which determine the policy of the capitalist state,
regardless of the dressing-up of these postulates in terms of
national interests or honor. This instinct of Soviet international
policy has contributed both to its strength and to its weakness.
It has endowed the Russian policy makers with a degree of
sophistication about international relations surpassing the old
platitudes of the diplomatic art; it has also, at times, made them
the dupes of the rigid dogmatisms they have erected to account
for the international situation. Thus the belated recognition of
the threat of Hitlerism which, according to a dogmatic oversimplification, should have proved but a prelude to a Communist revolution in Germany. Thus the initial underestimate

of the strength of national and democratic impulses which made the West stand up to Hitler, an underestimate which almost proved fatal to the Soviet Union. In a subsequent passage, I shall discuss what has happened in recent years to this Marxian technique of viewing the world outside the Soviet Union.

The second aspect of the legacy of Marxism to the policy makers of the Soviet Union is subtler and more paradoxical in its effect. Whereas the technique of viewing the world through the prism of Marxian categories of economic development and class conflict may be narrow and lead to serious miscalculations, it is still a rationalist technique. The other Marxian element is quasi-religious in its manifestations. It consists of an attachment to the symbols and phrases of the doctrine rather than to its analytical content. Just as in internal Soviet politics the official doctrine has been considered infallible and any errors or shortcomings in Soviet politics, economy, or culture have been attributed to mistakes or malevolence on the part of an individual, so in external relations the Soviet state has pursued the injunctions of Marxism-Leninism, and any departure from them (read a reversal in the foreign policy of the USSR) has been attributed to an individual's inability to apply Marxism-Leninism correctly to the given situation, or to his malice and treason. The terror of the Stalin era has been ascribed by his successors not to certain organic features of a totalitarian system, but solely to the pathological tendencies of the aging despot. When trying to re-establish a modus vivendi with Yugoslavia in the spring of 1955, Khrushchev felt constrained after arriving in Belgrade to blame the whole tangled story of the difficulties between the two states on the sinister malevolence of one man, Lavrenti Beria. To a Western commentator, grounded in the iconoclastic liberal tradition, the tendency of the Soviet leaders to invoke the magic formula of their doctrine as an explanation and guide to everything, *at the same time that they increasingly ignore and reject certain specific prescriptions of Marxism-Leninism,* smacks either of calculated hypocrisy or of a facile propaganda device. Yet such judgments are often oversimplified. The practitioners of the world's most totalitarian system must feel the need to believe in the infallibility of their doctrine; that the doctrine itself has become blurred or irrelevant to current situations does not change their tendency to use the magic incantation of Marxism. In both 1948 and 1958 in trying to account for their difficulties with Yugoslavia, the Soviets fell back upon the same ideological device: in 1948 the Yugoslav Communist Party was accused of the betrayal of Marxism-Leninism; in 1958, of revisionism. The whole complex of grievances against Tito and his regime has been reduced to an infraction of orthodoxy, of which the Communist Party of the Soviet Union is the only and infallible exponent. Three years of efforts by the Khrushchev regime to alter through diplomacy and compromise what they themselves had branded as Stalin's erroneous and paranoiac condemnation of the Yugoslavs ended in a milder version of the Stalinist fiat: since Yugoslavia is a source of trouble for the Soviet Union, since her anomalous position is in itself an open encouragement of independent-minded Communist satellites, the Yugoslavs obviously cannot be bona fide Communists. Once again the Soviets demonstrated that they cannot regard an international situation as essentially a series of concrete issues between states, but rather as an ideological conflict or betrayal.

If we think of the potential uses of Marxism for actual politics, we might separate three main strains: first, as a body of implied prescriptions (implied, because Marx and Engels never devoted much attention to the problem of the foreign policy of a socialist state); second, as an analytical discipline for viewing international as well as domestic politics; and, finally, as a symbol and quasi-religion giving its practitioners the sense that they are moving forward with the forces of history and that the success of their state is predicated upon the truth of the doctrine. It is asserted here that the first strain no longer plays any significant part in Soviet foreign policies, while the analytical and symbolical uses of Marxism remain important and necessary to the understanding of Soviet policy. In pondering the interconnection of the three elements of the ideological inheritance of the Soviet system, we are immediately struck by certain parallels to a society undergoing the process of secularization: when specific points of a religous creed lose their veracity or relevance for people, can they for long retain a general religious outlook and belief in the doctrine as a whole? Similarly, if the Marxian doctrine loses its specific relevance, can the frame of mind engendered by it and the belief itself endure? It is tempting for a Western observer to answer this question in the negative and to envisage a time when the realities of the world will bring about a reorientation of Soviet values. Kennan in his famous essay postulated the possibility of a change in the Soviet outlook consequent upon the failure of their assumptions about capitalism: "The palsied decrepitude of the capitalist world is the keystone of Communist philosophy. Even the failure of the United States to experience the early economic depression which the ravens of the Red Square have been predicting with such complacent confidence since hostilities ceased would have deep and important repercussions throughout the Communist world."[4] And further: "For no mystical Messianic movement—and particularly not that of the Kremlin—can face frustration indefinitely without eventually adjusting itself in one way or another to the logic of that state of affairs."[5]

Kennan overlooked, perhaps, the natural intransigence of religious millenarian movements to purely rational objective facts. *Credo quia absurdum* is not entirely atypical of the attitude of religious or political fanaticism. But the most fundamental objection to the postulating of an erosion of the ideology by contact with reality is that this ideology is propagated within a totalitarian system. If the rulers of this system see in the ideology, as we have seen, not only the rationale of their absolute power but a source of their inner security and effectiveness, then the doctrine will not be soon or easily repudiated just because the West increases its material welfare. Furthermore, while the Soviet citizen, including the indoctrinated party member, has numerous occasions to discover the contradictions or irrelevancies of Marxism in his daily life, he enjoys no such tangible experiences insofar as the world outside the USSR is concerned. And to the Soviet leaders, the field of foreign relations offers the best opportunity to attempt to demonstrate the viability of Marxism, conscious as they are of the necessity of preserving and developing the ideological élan of the Communist Party and of the regime. Marxism may be irrelevant to the problems of the Soviet Union now that its industrialization is accomplished and the state has shown no signs of withering away or becoming, in essence, less authoritarian. If some meaning is to be attached to the ideology, if it is not to fade out completely in the minds of the Soviet people, then it must show its effectiveness in propelling Soviet society into economic and scientific development at a *faster pace* than that achieved by societies inspired by the rival creed. And most important of all, the Soviet brand of Marxism must be shown to be advancing in the world at large, proving alluring to societies emerging from backwardness and colonial rule. The battle to preserve Soviet ideology in the USSR and with it the rationale of the totalitarian system is thus being fought in a world context, and the spread of Soviet ideology, influence, and prestige throughout the world becomes increasingly crucial to the preservation of the Soviet system as we know it.

The latter statement sounds like a truism. But we may best put it in perspective by contrasting the present situation with that which prevailed in the first decade after the revolution. The Russian Communists, a group devoted much more literally to their ideology than the current rulers of Russia, were confronted with the seeming failure of the ideological premises on which the revolution had been undertaken. It was only their own weak and backward country which remained under the rule of their version of socialism. Elsewhere in the world, the wave of revolutionary feeling had subsided and capitalism appeared to be stabilized. The logical response to the situation was to build the prerequisites of socialism in Russia; and the ideology was vindicated by the industrialization of the Soviet state. The terrible cost of the transformation and the increasingly ruthless totalitarian methods employed cannot obscure the fact that Marxism, and the ideological fervor generated by it, were crucial factors in the achievement. And, conversely, the achievement appeared to vindicate the ideology and the totalitarian system of the USSR. Today, it may be flatly asserted that the growth of the USSR can proceed on its own momentum. If the ideology is to become increasingly decorative and meaningless, in terms of concrete problems of Soviet life, where, in the last resort, will be the rationale for the totalitarian system, for the assumed omnipotence and omniscience of the highest councils of the Communist Party? The focus of "proving" Marxism-Leninism, and by the same token of preserving something of the old ideological élan and sense of mission, without which the most efficient totalitarian regime runs the danger of internal disintegration, has shifted once again beyond the geographical confines of the USSR.

II

To the outsider, the shifting trends of Soviet policy appear almost incomprehensible. The Khrushchev who in 1955 and 1956 proclaimed the legitimacy of seeking various roads to socialism is the same person who in the spring of 1958 led the attack upon the "revisionism" of the Yugoslav Communists.[6] In 1956, in his secret report on Stalin and Stalinism, Khrushchev bluntly blamed the Yugoslav situation on the pathological characteristics of the late despot.[7] And yet in 1958 the charge advanced against the Yugoslav Communist Party repeated many points of the Stalinist indictment of 1948–1949. The Yugoslavs indulged in revisionism by stressing the possibility of separate roads to socialism: they implied that the Soviet Union could also be guilty of increasing international tension, and such. As a matter of record, the Yugoslav party's program for its Seventh Congress in 1958 did not say anything that Tito and his group had not been saying before—and most of which had been acquiesced in by Khrushchev and his colleagues in 1955 and 1956. Even the charge that the Soviet Union was contributing to world tension had been acknowledged by Khrushchev, though blamed on Stalin, and the indictment against Molotov, Kaganovich, and Malenkov upon their expulsion from the Central Committee in July 1957 accused them of attempting as high officials of the Soviet Union to perpetuate international tensions. There is no phrase in the Yugoslav program the truth of which had not been conceded by the leadership of the Soviet Union during the preceding three years.

Explanations of this *volte-face* by the Soviet leadership have ranged from the alleged pressure exerted by the Chinese Communists on behalf of Communist orthodoxy, to the existence of a Stalinist group in the Central Committee which out of nostalgia for the late dictator and his policies continues to embarrass Khrushchev and compels him to resort to former policies and tactics. Yet there is no tangible evidence in support of either thesis.* True, attacks upon the Yugoslavs began to

---

* See on this problem my last essay, "Khrushchev and Boccaccio." Current (1962) Chinese attacks on Tito are obviously against the Russians' wishes.

appear in the Chinese Communist press before the Russians made a full-fledged attack. But it is perfectly natural that this should have occurred, if a joint attack upon Tito had been determined sometime before. Ever since the rise of Communist China, the satellites have looked upon it hopefully as the best means of eventually obtaining a modicum of independence from the Russians. Long after Yugoslavia's breach with the Russians in 1948, the Yugoslav press continued to extol Communist China. If once again the Yugoslav experiment had to be branded as unsocialist, and the satellites again called to task, it was sound strategy and psychology that the initiative should appear to come from China rather than from the USSR.

The notion of a Stalinist faction in the Presidium and the Central Committee also requires a qualification. As in any political and particularly any totalitarian situation, there is no doubt that the inside group at the summit of power in Russia is split up into, if not open, then latent factions. Every faction will exploit its opponents' failures, whether these failures are grounded in alleged "liberalism" or in alleged "Stalinism." But there is no evidence to indicate the existence of an outright Stalinist faction. The complex of methods of governing associated with Stalin is so abhorrent, even in the eyes of high party officials in the USSR, that it has been part of a sound psychological campaign by Khrushchev to brand his opponents as would-be renovators of Stalinism. It is clear, for example, that Malenkov, Molotov, and Kaganovich plotted against Khrushchev, and that during the winter of 1956–1957 they probably came close to replacing him by Shepilov or Pervukhin. But that they did so in the name of abstract Stalinism is as little probable and worthy of belief as the charge in their indictment that they opposed the USSR's attempting to catch up with and overtake the United States in the production of butter, milk, and meat.

The reasons for Russia's reversals of attitude toward Yugoslavia are to be sought in the reappraisal of policies toward the satellites which the Soviet leadership as a whole seems to have undertaken during recent years. The history of this reappraisal provides the best illustration of the interweaving of ideology, power motives, and internal politics in the making of Soviet foreign policy.

At the time of Stalin's death, Russian domination of the satellites was absolute and extended to the smallest details of their internal policies. Whatever changes the rulers were forced to make in the Stalinist pattern insofar as internal Soviet politics was concerned, there appeared no logical reason, granting their totalitarian premises, to change substantially the system of terror and close control which held Eastern Europe in subjugation to the USSR. Yet parallel with so-called liberalization in Soviet Russia, a new course was set in the satellites. Terror was relaxed and some semblance of internal autonomy was granted to the local Communists, who, at first incredulously, listened to their Russian masters urging them to do certain things on their own. Many satellite Communist leaders most closely associated with the Stalinist era of repression were either pushed to the second rank (Chervenkov in Bulgaria, Cepicka in Czechoslovakia, Berman in Poland, and others) or obligingly died (this being the case with Gottwald and Bierut). The highest party and state offices in the satellites were separated, and the local Stalins were either fired or told to share their power with a wider circle of party colleagues.[8] Soviet pressure for show trials of "deviationists" and other morbid paraphernalia of Communist statecraft of the Stalin era disappeared. For the first time since 1948, the satellite regimes enjoyed some power of decision on such issues as the pace of collectivization, cultural policies, and so on.

Now, it is easy to see in the new course of 1953–1956, which was not consistent and uniform insofar as all the European satellites of the USSR were concerned, the reflection of internal dissension and uncertainty within the Kremlin circle itself. But it is reasonably clear that the new policies represented a measure of consensus among the successors of Stalin. Just as in internal politics they decided to eliminate the most oppressive measures and techniques of Stalin, so in their relations with the satellites they tended to substitute the ties of mutual interest and ideology for the most stringent aspects of foreign control. In both cases, one of the main reasons was ideological. Stalin's techniques, his successors held, were partly pathological, partly obsolete in their severity. The maximum of control which they obtained did not compensate for the sapping of the vital forces of the Communist parties at home and abroad, for the impairing and tarnishing of the attraction of revolutionary socialism in the uncommitted parts of the world.

This ideological element was twofold in character. One side of the decision was the feeling that the Communist parties in the Soviet Union and the Soviet bloc could not be allowed to ossify and to become nothing but bodies of bureaucrats and spies driven by compulsion and ritualistic obeisances without, in the long run, creating a basic danger to the regime. The phrase "contact with the masses" is not used by the Communists entirely hypocritically. To give up some degree of control in exchange for popularity was deemed to be a reasonable gamble. The other side of the ideological element in the new course was the apparent conviction of the masters of the Kremlin that, when stripped of its worst excesses, Communism possessed enough historical truth and popular attraction to secure the devotion of even those who had suffered for years under its "errors." In the immemorial manner of politicians, the Soviet leaders assumed that they could have their cake and eat it, too; that the fundamental features of internal totalitarianism and essential control over the satellites could be preserved, and yet that the removal of the worst abuses would procure them genuine loyalty, would release new creative impulses and ideological fervor among the Communists at home and abroad.[9] In an ideological revival, Stalin's successors wanted to anticipate and forestall two great dangers. The first was that the gradual erosion of ideology through the continuance of methods of the Stalin era would strip the party entirely of its meaning and its esprit de corps. If that happened, the party, while nominally in existence and in power, could in fact be supplanted by another organization, the security apparatus or the army. In foreign affairs the prevalence of the 1948–1952 pattern of relations could lead to the second danger—the complete attenuation of ideological ties between the Communist Party of the USSR and the foreign Communists, whether in the satellites or in other countries. If that were to happen, what of the future relations of the USSR with the Communists in China, what of the loyalty of other Communists in the eventuality of a clash with the West? Thus what are, from the perspective of the West, rather intangible theoretical categories had for the Soviet leaders concrete ideological meaning readily translatable into considerations of power.

The new course in inter-Communist relations was thus to parallel the de-Stalinization at home. But on this count Stalin's successors, as they must have ruefully realized by the fall of 1956, fell into the very error of their dreaded predecessor. It was Stalin who applied without any inhibitions the methods he found workable in the USSR in dealing with non-Soviet Communists. And the post-Stalin regime, which by relaxation of terror reaped the dividends of a certain popularity and increased esprit de corps among the Communists and the population at large in the USSR, blithely expected the same results from similar policies in other Communist states. Stalin could be denounced and his regime in which the present rulers had been important figures could be revealed as having indulged in wholesale murder and atrocities, and yet the totalitarian structure could be preserved and Soviet Communism appear stronger for having acknowledged its errors. It appeared equally simple to proclaim Tito as having been unjustly denounced, Gomulka mistakenly imprisoned, and Rajk judicially murdered, and to expect a growth in the popularity of Communism and affection toward the USSR in Yugoslavia, Poland, and Hungary. Being intelligent men, the Soviet leaders must have expected some form of shock to result from the revelations and the institution of the new course, but, having been imprisoned within the Soviet system and within their own ideological premises for forty years, they evidently did not expect that the shock would take the form of revulsion toward Communism, demoralization of local Communist parties, and even open hostility toward the Soviet Union.

Having decided upon the modification of Stalinist practices, the Soviet leaders proceeded boldly. The visit of Khrushchev and Bulganin to Belgrade in the spring of 1955 was a stroke of diplomacy as startling in terms of what had gone before as would have been a visit of Eisenhower and Dulles to Peking or of Macmillan and Selwyn Lloyd to Cairo. But quite apart from the assumed humility of the Russians toward the man and regime they had tried for years to overthrow, and against which they had hurled the most fantastic accusations and insults, the visit dramatized the importance attached by the Soviet Union to the principle of the ideological unity of the Communist world. Again, being realists, the Soviet leaders must have realized that the Communists in the satellites would draw their own conclusions from this bowing in effect to the defier of Stalin. A premium would be put upon a certain amount of nationalist intransigence, and the Communists of Poland or Rumania would no longer be terrified of standing up to their Soviet colleagues. But if the Yugoslav gamble worked, what was lost in absoluteness of control would be counterbalanced by the growth of genuine ideological unity. Soviet Russia could resume the ideological and diplomatic offensive in Asia and Africa without a Communist state standing as visible proof that the USSR was dominated by imperialist rather than ideological motives. To liquidate the Yugoslav defection this time through diplomacy became one of the main Soviet objectives, and the reasons for it are to be found not only in the "propaganda" aspects of Soviet foreign policy but in the need for ideological self-assurance. An outside observer may have from the beginning foreseen the gross psychological error inherent in the method of rapprochement with Tito. He may have argued, as undoubtedly some had argued in the Politburo, that a more gradual and cautious re-establishment of friendly relations with Yugoslavia would have produced less of a shock on the satellites (and the same observation applies to the unmasking of Stalin by Khrushchev). Yet one is left with some appreciation of the boldness of the move and of the new demonstration of the flexibility of Soviet policy. The policy initiated by the post-Stalin Presidium had, however, this distinguishing characteristic: it freely envisaged the abandonment of a certain amount of control—something the old despot had been unwilling to do—in the expectation of considerable ideological gains.

Khrushchev and his colleagues, then, took a fairly long-run point of view: the Communist bloc would be reconstructed, this time with Yugoslavia as a valued member. Day-to-day control of the satellites' affairs would be abandoned by the Russians, but foreign and defense policies would be more effectively synchronized with those of the USSR. Their internal sovietization would proceed ever so much more intensely and healthily, now that it was not being accomplished under extreme duress. The new policies would obviate, or at least postpone, a clash with the Chinese Communists which would have been unavoidable had the old Stalinist policies been rigidly adhered to. The united Communist bloc would be much more attractive to the new uncommitted nations, and Asian and

African leftists would not have the dismaying example of the Soviet-Yugoslav dispute to dampen their pro-Communist inclinations. Finally, within the Soviet Union, the fact that the Communist states were united and more freely associated on the international scene would help in the ideological reactivation of Communism in Russia.

Within two years the main premise of the new Soviet policies was exposed as hollow. The tie of ideology did not prove strong enough to hold the Communist bloc together and subservient to Russia in the absence of more tangible means of control. The return of Yugoslavia to the Soviet bloc could not simply obliterate the seven years during which the Yugoslav leaders had learned to be independent. For ideological and power reasons of his own, Tito was only too glad to arrive at a modus vivendi with the Russians. The continued isolation from the Communist bloc was slowly undermining the morale of the Yugoslav party, the main support of his totalitarian regime, as witnessed by the Djilas affair. But the Yugoslavs could not now settle for what they would gladly have taken from Stalin in 1948: internal autonomy, but in other respects unquestioning adherence to the USSR. This time the Yugoslavs were ready to re-enter the Soviet bloc only as representatives and propagators of the idea of equality of socialist states. The Soviet Union as the leading socialist state would still enjoy primacy, but each member of the bloc should be granted external and internal independence. What was implicit in the Soviet *theory* of the new course the Yugoslavs were eager to make explicit in *practice*.

The imperfect reconciliation became an additional disruptive influence within the Soviet sphere. The events of October 1956 represented a serious blow to Soviet policies. Again the policy habit acquired within the Soviet context proved almost disarmingly naive when applied to another country. It was easy for the Russians to imagine that, with the worst repression abolished in Poland and the deviant Communists rehabilitated, Soviet influence would be made more secure and Polish Communism would become even more loyal to the USSR. But Gomulka was not only readmitted to the Communist Party but was carried to power, and the Polish army passed from the control of Soviet officers. Finally, the events of Hungary demonstrated vividly that not only Soviet influence but Communism in Eastern Europe rests mainly upon force, and that any weakening in the network of Soviet controls and terror would not readily be compensated by an enhanced ideological solidarity with the Soviet Union. It is not too much to assume that the events in Eastern Europe had a certain unsettling effect upon the Russian Communists, and that their intellectual and artistic side effects, which spilled over the borders of the Soviet Union, went in the opinion of the leaders beyond the legitimate and safe limits of liberalization.

The balance sheet of the new policy was therefore largely negative. But it is instructive to see that the Soviets did not panic at the failure of their design. We have no means of knowing what discussions went on in Moscow after the Polish and Hungarian events. But it is unlikely that the Soviets would have or could have implemented the policy of complete return to Stalinism either in their internal affairs or in dealing with Eastern Europe. The pendulum had swung too far, and the decision was taken in the winter of 1956–1957 to restore a form of balance between the old and the new policies. It was hoped that the fortieth anniversary of the October Revolution in 1957 would see the beginning of a new Communist International to replace the Cominform, dissolved in 1956 as a relic of the Stalinist era and discredited in its only major undertaking: the attempt to undermine and overthrow Tito. The Cominform had been organized in the summer of 1947 mainly to give an international appearance to the Soviet control of the Communist parties in power, and thus to obviate the trouble which the

Russians already discerned in the Yugoslav situation.[10] Now, in a different atmosphere the new Communist organization, in which various ruling and perhaps other Communist parties would associate in apparent equality, would again give an international appearance to Soviet guidance. But, as we know, the Yugoslav Communists for obvious reasons refused to participate in a new Cominform. Their refusal, it seems, was supported by the Poles, and thus for the time being no international Communist agency could be created to "internationalize" Soviet control of the satellites' policies. The new method of "domesticating" Tito proved no more successful than the previous ones. Furthermore, the carrier of the Titoist virus had again been taken into the Communist camp as a bona fide member, visiting the satellite capitals and entertaining in Yugoslavia delegations of the Polish, Hungarian, and Rumanian Communists.

It is in the light of these developments that the Soviet decision to denounce the Yugoslav Communists, in terms considerably milder than those of 1948, becomes understandable. If in 1948 Tito and his group were denounced as followers of Bukharin and Vollmar, and then as agents of Western imperialism, they became in 1958 revisionists and fence-sitters. Again obscure doctrinal excommunications were pronounced by the Soviet Communists to account for the failure to solve their own ideological dilemma: how can an international political movement be genuinely international and yet be run and controlled by a single state?* And that problem is but the other side of the internal dilemma: how can you have ideological fervor and socialist élan in a totalitarian and bureaucratic state? These seemingly intangible theoretical questions appear to the Soviet leaders with the increasing urgency of problems of

---

* The most recent and most drastic reverberations of the problem—the developments concerning China and Albania—are discussed in my concluding essay.

power. It is almost pathetic to observe the Russians attempting to develop within the last few years some of the paraphernalia of popular government. Stalin never went abroad, with the exception of the wartime trip to Teheran. The current leaders travel assiduously, especially in the satellite areas. They do not confine themselves, as was the pre-1953 pattern, to conferences with high state and party officials. They address themselves to crowds. The visit of Voroshilov to Poland in the spring of 1958 was an exhibition of the new technique. The aged titular head of the USSR visited factories, farms, and party gatherings. He was accompanied by a retinue of dignitaries, including—most significantly—high officials of the Byelorussian, Ukrainian, and Lithuanian parties, who shared in the frantic visiting and speech making. It is unlikely that this search for popularity will lead the Russians to put it to test by removing the more tangible forms of insurance of their satellites' loyalty. Veiled threats accompany professions of ideological brotherhood, as during Khrushchev's tour of Hungary. But in the speeches and activities connected with the satellites there has definitely been a new tone since 1955: an attempt by the Soviet leaders to convince not only others but, one might almost say, themselves that the Communist commonwealth of states is based upon ideological ties rather than upon force or threats of force. Even the reversal of the new course, the stiffened Soviet attitude toward manifestations of satellite "nationalism," does not change that tendency basically.

The problem of working out a feasible pattern of relations between the states in the "camp of socialism" is increasingly becoming one of the main problems of Soviet policy, and not only of *foreign* policy. The earlier attempted solution—strict subordination by force—has proved impractical, and, no matter how much is said about the return to Stalinism, the situation prior to 1953 simply cannot be reproduced. Enough of Marxist historical sophistication remains in the rulers of the Kremlin to prevent them from attempting to turn back history. Not because of any increased humanitarianism, but because of changed conditions, they will try to supplement force with diplomacy and with an increased community of interests between themselves and their satellites. Much has been said about the "erosion" of Soviet ideology, but ideologies and social movements are not eroded by the mere passage of time or the impact of statistics. Nineteenth-century liberalism was eroded, and with it much of the influence of the West in other parts of the world, largely by the abrasive force of nationalism. Communism has up to now managed to turn this abrasive force to its own uses, but it has begun to experience its unsettling effect within its own system.

III

The example of Soviet policy within the Communist bloc is perhaps sufficient to point out the involved nature of the ideological element in the policy as a whole. The contribution of the ideology is not simply to endow the Soviet rulers with a propensity for violence and conquest. Nor is Marxism-Leninism an unsubstantial line of fortifications separating the Soviet Union from the rest of the world, quite ready to collapse at repeated trumpetings of the facts of the West's material and political stability and peaceful intentions toward the USSR. Soviet ideology, in the sense discussed here, is neither a detailed guide to action nor a superficial creed vulnerable to exposure. Quite apart from its textual content, belief in this ideology represents the most cohesive force in the Soviet system, one which has enabled Communist Party rule and the dynamics of industrialization to persist through decades of oppression, misrule, and economic suffering. It has been observed that Communist ideology now has but little relevance insofar as domestic problems of the Soviet Union are concerned. Were the USSR to cease being a one-party state equipped with totalitarian paraphernalia, the process of industrialization and modernization would go on under the aegis of another ideology and another political system. There has been no change or reform in the social or economic field in the last ten years which might not have been effected in the USSR for purely pragmatic reasons. If the ideology is to remain demonstrably important to the Soviet citizen, and demonstrably correct to the party members—and the perpetuation of the Communist Party rule rests in the long run upon these assumptions—then there must be a dimension other than the domestic one in which Communist ideology does make a difference. Successful proselytizing becomes an important factor in the preservation of the faith. Foreign successes, the preservation and expansion of collaboration within the Communist bloc, become important insofar as the preservation of the present pattern of Communism in the USSR is concerned.

If this hypothesis is correct, then there is little foundation in the hope often expressed in the West that the growth and maturity of the USSR as a modern and industrial state will necessarily be reflected in more peaceful and less expansive policies. As we have seen, the growing power and prosperity of the USSR *as a state*, even the increased material well-being of its citizens, accentuate rather than diminish the ideological crisis. This ideological crisis is not, as so often imagined, simply the matter of whether the everyday reality of Soviet life conforms to the precepts of Marx and Lenin, but of the existence and growth of social and economic forces which impinge upon the foundations of the totalitarian system in Russia. At the height of the collectivization struggle, Stalin propounded his famous formula, then the rationalization for the ruthless suppression of the peasants, that the closer the goal of socialism, the sharper the character of the class struggle. This terrible formula, pronouncing in effect that more success will necessitate more terror, was declared un-Marxist by Stalin's successors.[11] But it unwittingly contained an important insight; in the measure that the Communist movement achieves its objectives, it becomes increasingly difficult to preserve the totalitarian system, to continue to exact sacrifices and deny basic freedoms and amenities of life. The program of ideological revival devised by the despot's successors has aimed at preventing Communism from "withering away," and thus at preserving the rationale of Soviet totalitarianism. A great part in this revival has been played by the renewed missionary character of Communism. Thus the success of Communism as a self-proclaimed world-wide liberation and peace movement, and as a tenable basis for the association of Communist states, becomes increasingly important to the continuance of the present form of the Communist regime in the USSR.

Most studies of Soviet foreign policy imply or state the question: what can the West do about it? And in the process of asking this question, we very often and unavoidably distort the problem according to our hopes or fears, or indulge in a natural irritation because the drift of world affairs has not gone according to our plans and expectations. I have attempted here to sketch the connection between Soviet ideology, so different now and yet descended in many ways from the prototypes of Marxism and Leninism, and actual Soviet policies. All that a study of this kind can do is to suggest a certain range of problems and characteristics of Russian policies. It cannot, nor can the most detailed scheme of the politics of the USSR, predict the eventuality of either a peaceful resolution of the East-West conflict or its catastrophic settlement. Nor is it possible to sketch an "unavoidable" pattern of development of Soviet policies either toward a repetition of the Stalinist pattern or toward an erosion of totalitarianism. Very often in our analyses we tend to be more deterministic than our antagonists are.

Yet, within a shorter range of time and without attempting to answer the really unanswerable and, alas, most important questions, it is possible to outline some basic difficulties of the

Soviet international position. It has been suggested here that the ideological crisis created, paradoxically, by the successes of the Communist system impels it to seek a justification of the ideology in the international sphere. Thus, and not only because of the natural tendency of a totalitarian system, the USSR is bent upon ideological and power expansion. Here we encounter one of those "inherent contradictions" with which the Marxists upbraid the capitalist system, but of which their own offers glittering examples. Just as within the Soviet Union the reality of a modernized and industrialized society clashes with the ideological premises, and the contradiction is encompassed only by the chains of totalitarianism, so within the Communist bloc the reality of Soviet domination clashes with the ideological premise of the equality of socialist states; the contradiction is concealed (imperfectly, as Yugoslavia, Hungary, and Poland have demonstrated) only by an enormous preponderance of power, which is for the time being on the side of the USSR. Here, then, are the Algerias and Cypruses of the Soviet camp, and the proverbial forces of history that appear to be working for the Russians in disrupting the liberal world are impinging upon the combination of socialism and totalitarianism which is Soviet ideology.

4 THE NEW FACE OF SOVIET TOTALITARIANISM

Nothing pricks one's curiosity more than the inner operations of a power system. And in the case of Russia the incentive to speculate on "what really goes on" in the councils of the Kremlin is enhanced by the supersecrecy in which the highest level of Soviet politics is enveloped, by the dramatic shifts of policy and sudden displacements of leading personalities, and by a natural apprehension about the operations of a totalitarian regime which may at any moment threaten or transform our daily lives.

In the United States, the mechanics of power in the Soviet Union have become a matter of national interest. A television show not too long ago undertook to recreate the events leading to Stalin's death. The public is frequently invited by the press to ponder the significance of the replacement of a security chief in Kazakhstan or a party secretary in Georgia. Newspaper stereotypes of leading Soviet figures appear almost as often as those of American presidential possibilities. Who has not heard of "ebullient" Nikita Khrushchev? And we have been

SOURCE: First published in *World Politics*, April 1960.

presented with his potential rival: the "dour ideologue," Mikhail Suslov. As if in ironic expiation of the national sin of isolationism, the American people are concerning themselves increasingly with the fortunes of the Kirichenkos, Molotovs, and Zhukovs, and the activities and motivations of those distant political figures weigh heavily upon the national consciousness.

And yet how tenuous the basis upon which we erect our hypotheses and conjectures about Soviet politics! Unlike the performers in some other television shows, actors in the drama dealing with Stalin's death could have no assurance that their lines adhered to historical truth. That Suslov is a potential rival of Khrushchev or that Malenkov and Molotov were removed because of their attachment to Stalin's policies and methods are conjectures based, respectively, upon an unverifiable assumption and upon a charge which they have been in no position to answer. We have no right to scoff at these conjectures, but we must look for more solid bits of evidence before we try to construct a realistic picture of politics in the Soviet Union.

I

Fortunately, we are now beginning to acquire more in the way of concrete material than visitors' conversations with the Soviet leaders or the Pythian language of the official Communist pronouncements. The flow of post-Stalin politics in Russia has forced some facts to emerge from behind the closed doors of the Kremlin, some degree of deliberation or decision making to be done in public. In a step fairly unprecedented in recent years, the Soviet rulers deemed fit to release the minutes of the Central Committee meeting (the plenum, as the official phraseology has it) which took place in December 1958. We have in our hands not only, as in the case of the usual Central Committee meeting, the resolution and the speech of the rapporteur, most frequently the First Secretary of the party, but also minutes of all speeches delivered.[1]

To be sure, our find contains no sensational revelations. The committee met and deliberated in an atmosphere completely dominated by Khrushchev. Hence the decision to publish the proceedings. We would give a great deal for the minutes of the meeting which in 1953 removed Beria and his associates, or of the plenum of June 1957, when Malenkov, Molotov, Kaganovich, and Shepilov were disgraced and Khrushchev's supremacy firmly established. The proceedings of December 1958 were published and widely circulated exactly because they bore witness to the consolidation and unity of the Central Committee and offered an account—not fully reliable—of the sins of the defeated oppositionists which had allegedly led to their expulsion. But if there is no lurid revelation, we are still presented with a document of great importance. The Central Committee examined *the* problem of Soviet society and politics: the development of and future plans for Soviet agriculture. From both what was said and what can be inferred, we gain an insight into the current state of Soviet totalitarianism.

Take an incident of rather secondary importance. Most of the plenum was devoted to the reports of the local party secretaries as to the conditions and prospects of agriculture in their republics and regions. Thus the secretary of the Azerbaijan Communist Party, Mustafayev, reports on his country. All is not well with collectivized agriculture in this Transcaucasian republic. The party satrap is embarrassed to confess that the peasants cling to private ownership of cattle and that even special taxes are not effective in making them sell their cows, sheep, and goats to the kolkhozes. "And can't you educate them in the principles of socialist agriculture?" asks Khrushchev. "True, Nikita Sergeyevich, but we need time." "And how much time do you need? Haven't forty-one years of Soviet power been enough?" [2] Mustafayev tries to divert the discussion from his peasants and their perverse intransigence to Marxism-Leninism: rumors have reached him of a disquieting state of affairs in Soviet agronomy. Have not some professors attacked that great pioneer of Marxism in biology, Trofim Lysenko? A member of a Soviet scientific delegation to Peiping even had the gall to say: "We are done not only with Lysenko's theories, but with his methods as well." [3] "It is Tsitsin who said it," remarks Khrushchev, indicating how extensive are his sources of information and how injudicious it is to be indiscreet even five thousand miles from Moscow. "Call him before a Party meeting, and ask him as a Party member how he could have said it."

Mustafayev's talents in changing the subject of conversation did not avail him for long. The Azerbaijan peasants must have persisted in their un-Marxist attachment to their cows and goats, for in June 1959 he was sacked as the boss of Azerbaijan. No lesser rising star of the party than Semichastny, until then the head of the Komsomol, was dispatched to become the second secretary* of the republic party (the first secretaryship and the titular leadership went, as custom now demands, to a native)—a fact that indicates the importance which the highest circles of the USSR attach to the problem.

The incident is symptomatic of a significant characteristic of Soviet politics: the ability to tread the line laid down by the party and personal loyalty to Khrushchev are not enough in themselves to save an important official from disgrace. What is demanded is performance. The party has set itself an enormous task of expansion in the sector of the national economy which has lagged under the Soviet rule, agriculture. A pseudoscientific charlatan like Lysenko is restored to favor not improbably because he promises quick and sensational results from his methods of improving breeds and increasing output. Lysenko, whose ejection from his position as the dictator of Soviet biological sciences was a logical sequence of the official denigration of Stalin and the cult of personality, was allowed at the

---

* He is now the head of the Committee of State Security (secret police).

plenum to denounce distinguished Soviet scientists who disagreed with his methods, and, if he was not restored to his previous position, he was licensed to practice his charlatanry in a new direction: livestock breeding.

But this is only one of many devices and improvisations snatched at by the party and the regime in their haste to raise the agricultural output. Ideological and political aims have become inextricably tied up with economic ones. It is not inappropriate to compare this meeting of the Central Committee of the Communist Party to a meeting of the board of a huge corporation. The regional directors render their accounts, the stories of their successes, problems, and difficulties. From time to time the leading "salesmen"—the collective farmers and agronomists—are called upon to intersperse the dignitaries' speeches with reports of successful new techniques and improvisations whose adoption would raise output and enable the USSR to outdistance the competitor. The chairman of the board is clearly in command of the whole enterprise. Nikita Khrushchev interrupts the others' speeches, cracks jokes, and deals out praise and reprimands. But even he works under the same compulsion as his subordinates. Even his position in the party is not uninfluenced by the indices of production or independent of the successes and failures of the campaign to expand Russia's production and consumption of foodstuffs.

The complex of problems connected with the peasant-agriculture nexus has always been at the heart of Russian politics. It has fallen to Khrushchev to confirm what Western economists have known or suspected for a long time: at the end of the Stalin era, Soviet agriculture had reached a serious crisis. "In fact," said the First Secretary, "the country insofar as the production of grain was concerned found itself at the *same level as prerevolutionary Russia*." [4] After thirty-five years of socialism and twenty years of collectivization, Soviet agriculture produced for a much greater population not much more than had backward Russia of 1910–1914. A prodigious increase in industrial production; stagnation and setbacks in agriculture—such has been, to borrow a Marxist term, the inherent contradiction of the Soviet system.

What are the reasons and where is the blame to be allotted? We cannot expect the First Secretary to say that the collective system goes against the instincts of the Soviet peasant, that the Soviet regime as a whole has erred in carrying the exploitation of its rural population to a point where oppression becomes not only brutal but also uneconomical and self-defeating. There are obvious and convenient culprits. It is the antiparty group, comrades ("And one's speech falters at calling them comrades, though they are still in the Party," says Khrushchev), Malenkov, Molotov, Kaganovich, and Shepilov, who bear the responsibility for this sorry plight, and who until their ejection in 1957 opposed every positive and helpful measure to relieve the agricultural distress. Did not Malenkov lie when he asserted in 1952 that the country had harvested 8 billion poods of grain? He knew, since he was then in charge of agriculture, that the actual harvest was in fact 5.6 billion poods.[5] Did not Molotov propose to increase the quota for subscription to the national loan among the peasants, knowing full well that the peasants simply could not meet the increased quota and that the only result would be the worsening of political morale among the collective farmers? Did not the opposition as a whole scoff at and oppose every attempt to ameliorate the lot of the peasants, every attempt to open new lands for cultivation?

Thus Khrushchev. The defeated leaders are not present to give their side of the story. They take their place in the history of the party alongside the Trotskyites, who allegedly sabotaged the First Five-Year Plan; the Bukharinites, who mixed nails with butter and slaughtered livestock to discredit collectivization; the "people's enemy," Beria, who sent thousands of innocent Communists to their death; and that half-great, half-guilty man, Stalin, who invented terror and the cult of personality. As from Khrushchev's secret speech, so from his agricultural report somber facts emerge about the Soviet system, no matter where the blame is laid. Thus in 1953 serious trouble was avoided only through the use of the state reserves of foodstuffs, the current production being insufficient for basic needs.[6] The state loans stand revealed as another form of taxation—which is no surprise to the foreign experts. It is officially confirmed that the Soviet statistics were often falsified, the most common method in agriculture being the substitution of the biological yield for the grain actually collected and usable. But the connection of the antiparty group with the alleged misdeeds requires more careful examination because, among other things, in the process we shall perceive some interesting facts about Soviet politics.

Was Malenkov in 1952 the party official primarily responsible for Soviet agriculture? The falsified figures which Khrushchev quotes are drawn from the general report delivered at the Nineteenth Party Congress by Malenkov in his capacity as deputy for Stalin, a report which touched on almost every aspect of domestic and foreign policies. The report was made in the name of the Politburo and the Central Committee. It would be foolish to suppose that Malenkov's colleagues on those two bodies, certainly on the Politburo, did not know the real facts. Who as late as 1951 was the Politburo member assumed to be principally concerned with agriculture? None other than Nikita Khrushchev.

We shall get closer to the truth if we go back to the event which marks the real beginning in the post-Stalin development of Soviet agriculture, the plenum of the Central Committee of September 1953. It was this plenum which charted the new course to be adopted toward the peasant and which, incidentally, elevated Khrushchev to the position of First Secretary. It was he who delivered the report and outlined the steps to be taken in the future.[7] The story he told then was considerably different in tone, if not in substance, from the angry evaluation he was to render in 1958. No evocation of a danger of famine. No attribution of personal blame to Malenkov, who was then still the first man of the regime. No, the story of collectivized agriculture was depicted as one of progress and success. Figures were quoted warily by Khrushchev, something we can now understand. But he did quote them to assert that the commercial production of grain had grown fourfold between 1926/27 and 1952/53, and that the latter year marked a 10 percent increase in output over 1940.

The cat was let partially out of the bag when Khrushchev came to indicating the measures needed for further and greater successes. Here the tone of urgency was unmistakable. The party had neglected the use of material incentives in dealing with the peasant. The collective farmer's private plot had been assailed and threatened, thus further lowering his morale and his incentive to work. The concrete proposals by the rapporteur that were adopted by the Central Committee included an immediate rise in prices for agricultural products, a reduction in the compulsory supplies furnished by the kolkhozes to the state at fixed prices, and a considerable outlay of capital on agriculture and on improving the peasant's living conditions. A reader of *Pravda* might have been curious to know who in the past had been assailing the private plot, who had advocated solving the agricultural lag through greater centralization and discipline rather than through increased incentives and reassurances to the peasant. He would not have had to search his memory very strenuously to remember that Nikita Khrushchev had been under Stalin one of the people most directly concerned with collective-farm affairs, most active in the amalgamation of the farms into larger units, the man who in 1950 had advocated still further amalgamation into agrogorods—the agricultural cities. The most immediate result of the introduction of the agrogorods—where the peasants were to dwell in apartment houses and be driven out to the fields to work in brigades—would have been the abolition of the private plot. Even in the atmosphere of gigantomania and greater and greater centralization and compulsion which characterized the last years of Stalin, Khrushchev's proposal was deemed extravagant and impractical and was dropped by the party. But it was the same hand which had raised the stick over the peasant's head in 1950 which was now extending a carrot, the same man who had urged the extreme of compulsion who was now castigating past harshness and exactions.

But the important thing about the plenum of 1953, just as of that of 1958, was not the zigzag course adopted by Khrushchev or his callisthenics in shifting to others the blame for policies he himself had been largely responsible for. The important thing is to perceive how the agriculture-peasant nexus embodies the main dilemma of Soviet totalitarianism. What is the essence of the problem? Let us again listen to Khrushchev, this time in 1958. In speaking of the great progress made since 1953 in livestock breeding, he inserts the following qualification:

I would like to speak about one group of regions of the Russian republic, the leaders of which have not been up to the task, and consequently those regions are not listed among the leading ones, *though they have contributed a high percentage of the increase of the production of meat by the economy of the region as a whole. Can we measure success solely by this indicator? No, we cannot . . .* As is well known, the basic producers of meat for consumption are in our country the kolkhozes and sovkhozes . . . *Therefore, no matter how high the increase of production of meat as a whole, if the share of this increase contributed by the kolkhozes and sovkhozes is insignificant one has to say this region lags behind.* And such is the state of affairs in the above-mentioned regions. The Pskov region increased its meat production by 20 thousand tons, but its kolkhozes and sovkhozes only by 3.1 thousand tons . . .[8]

Here then is the classical dilemma: the peasant works more efficiently on his own, be it in his miserable plot or with his own fowls or cow, than as a member of a team in the socialized sector of the agricultural economy. The regime cannot accept the growth of production as satisfactory in itself if there is evidence that this growth is faster in the private than in the socialized sector. And the problem is not confined only to production; it reflects, as Khrushchev himself amply illustrates, a basic factor of the peasant's psychology. We have mentioned Mustafayev's sad case and how the inability of socialized cows and goats to breed as quickly as their privately owned fellow creatures can handicap the career of a powerful official. Here is additional evidence: "In some regions the number of cows grows because of the increase in the number of livestock owned privately by the peasants, workers and functionaries. *At the same time, the number of cows owned by the kolkhozes or sovkhozes either remains the same or decreases.* For instance, in the Astrakhan region in 1953 there were 37 thousand collectively and state-owned cows, and now there are only 35 thousand. But the number of cows owned by the individual peasants, workers, and functionaries has grown by 17 thousand." [9] The First Secretary goes on to support his complaints with several similar examples, which illustrate that for all the state and party support given to the collectivized sector, for all the meagerness of the actual acreage owned privately in household plots, for all the impossibility of an individual in the USSR owning a *considerable* number of cattle or fowls, the peasant continues to "vote" for more economic freedom, or at least a loosening of the collective structure.

The regime cannot allow him to push too far in that direction. In trying to give the peasant material and psychological incentives, the party under Khrushchev's leadership has considerably relaxed the iron clamp of centralization (at least insofar as administration, if not policy making, is concerned) and exploitation of the peasantry. In addition to the measures indicated above, the regime in 1958 allowed the collective farms to purchase the machine tractor stations. Here is what Stalin had to say in 1952 regarding the possibility of such a step:

The result, first, would be that the collective farms would become the owners of the chief tools of production. That is, they would attain an exceptional position, such as no enterprise in our country enjoys, since as is well known even the nationalized enterprises in our country are not the owners of the tools of production. How could one justify this exceptional position of the collective farms, by what consideration of progress or advance? Could one say that such a situation would be conducive to raising collective farm property to the level of public property, that it would speed the transition of our society from socialism to communism? Would it not be more accurate to say that such a situation could only further separate collective farm ownership from public ownership and lead us not closer to communism, but on the contrary further from it?[10]

Khrushchev chose to disregard Stalin's warning. The machine tractor station not only provided the collective farm with machinery, but also controlled and dictated the economic activity of the kolkhoz, and its personnel not infrequently has exerted political and police supervision as well. By turning it over to the collectives, the regime no doubt has thought to give the peasants a feeling of control over their economic activities (while still retaining to a great extent its own power of direction) and more of a sense of being members of a real *collective* farm rather than state employees tilling the land. But economic freedom in agriculture, leading to a pronounced difference in status between the peasant and the city worker, is very far from being an objective of the regime. It is clear that in Khrushchev's mind even the collective farm chained and directed by the state, as it still is in many ways, is no ideal form of agricultural organization. The settling and cultivation of the virgin lands have been done predominantly through the agency of the state farm, where the difference between the worker and peasant tends to be obliterated. For all the announced aims of surpassing the United States in the production of butter, milk, and meat, it is not likely that the First Secretary would listen with favor if by some miracle the Soviet economists were to say to him: "Nikita Sergeyevich, we have considered the problem and reached the unanimous conclusion that our agricultural production would double if we were to abolish state farms, loosen the remaining controls over the collective farms, and increase the size of the household plot."

The revulsion from anything which smacks of real economic freedom for the peasant, even if the price paid for this revulsion is the delay or hampering of the party's most cherished economic goals, is deeply grounded in the Communist ideology. It is important to understand what "ideology" means in this connection. It is not because of any superstitious reverence for the letter of Marxism or Leninism that the party will never give up collectivization and would always, ideally, prefer state to collective farms. On numerous occasions, and in many aspects of Soviet life, the original gospel has been unabashedly altered or abandoned. A keen sense of pragmatism, a freedom from fanatical dogmatism, has characterized Khrushchev's ascendance, and one has only to look at Russian society in the 1920s and mid-1930s to see that the same quality, in a different sense, was not lacking in Stalin. But that private property in agriculture is bad is not only something that the party leaders have learned from Marx, Lenin, and Stalin; it is something that they feel in their bones as a threat to their power, their position, and the whole rationale of the totalitarian system which they are bent on maintaining, even if in a modified and more rational form.

But almost as strong as that fear is the desire to expand

production in foodstuffs. The regime is determined "to catch up and surpass" the United States not only in heavy industry but in the absolute and relative production of foodstuffs. Again, in appraising the reasons for this aim it is impossible to separate neatly factors of ideology, economics, and the Soviet brand of power politics. Ideologically, the aim is to "prove" to the Soviet people that Communism not only is adept at industrialization, and especially at building heavy industry, but is equally capable and solicitous of raising the standard of living. Economically, without considerable improvement in agriculture, industrial progress itself might be threatened. And, politically, what more attractive "platform" could Khrushchev offer in attempting to consolidate his power, what better argument to the wavering or doubtful members of the Central Committee, than the promise of a better life for the masses—something which apart from its inherent appeal makes life easier for a party or state administrator?

In the economic—especially agricultural—field, we thus see another of those glittering "inherent contradictions" which the Marxist masters of the USSR are so want to find in the West. "Socialist legality" is proclaimed to disassociate Communism from the horrors of Stalinism and to infuse the party and the system with new vigor. But this legality may not advance to the point where something like a real rule of law is possible, for the regime is determined to keep its powers of repression. The area of intellectual freedom may be somewhat expanded, for again the old type of socialist realism and conformity were found to be stultifying and the breeders of boredom and hence dissatisfaction. But the loosening of the reins can never go so far as to permit genuine intellectual freedom, for a book like *Doctor Zhivago* with its antimaterialist message is much more of a threat to the ethos of Communism than any out-and-out attack upon the Soviet system would be. Similarly in agriculture: the need to give the peasant a reassurance that he will not be arbitrarily transformed into an urbanized wage earner, and that the few vestiges of his private property in land and stock will not be seized, clashes with the realization that even a small degree of economic independence for the peasants may place them in a position to threaten the absolute control of economic life which for the Communists is a matter of life or death.

It is against the canvas of these contradictions that the political game at the highest level takes place in the USSR. One of the sins attributed to the "antiparty gang" of Malenkov, Molotov, and Kaganovich has been their unwillingness to subscribe to the slogan of surpassing the United States in the production of the basic foodstuffs. It would be hard to imagine Molotov getting up and saying, "No, comrades, it would be dangerous for us to produce more milk per head than they do in America." But, as it emerges from the December plenum, the oppositionists felt that Khrushchev's targets were somewhat unrealistic—an opinion shared by several Western economists, who presumably have no stake in or sentimental attachment to Stalinism. It is not difficult to imagine Molotov and Kaganovich decrying Khrushchev's aims as demagogic, conducive to the raising of expectations whose disappointment would threaten the regime, if not the party, or whose fulfillment would require a diversion of resources from investment in producer goods. If Molotov did attack the plan of settlement and cultivation of the virgin lands as uneconomic, he had as company several Western experts on Soviet agriculture. The project, a key point in Khrushchev's plan of agricultural expansion, has meant the conversion to agriculture of vast areas of Kazakhstan and Siberia, previously thought unsuitable for cultivation. In the long run, the experts and Molotov apparently agree, those lands because of the dryness and salinity of their soil and other climatic factors may not justify the effort and expense.[11]

In the long run—but for an ambitious and determined politician, in the USSR as elsewhere, politics consists of a series of short-run situations. If the expansion of the area of cultivation can dramatically improve the total picture for a time, as it already has, what does it matter if the reclaimed areas eventually relapse into dust bowls? Helped by a couple of bumper crops, Khrushchev has been able to confound and eject his enemies. If and when their misapprehensions become substantiated, *they* will not be in a position to challenge the First Secretary, who will have in the meantime fastened his grip more firmly upon the party organization.

II

"And now it is the turn of Bulganin to speak." Thus the chairman of the session referred without the customary prefix of "Comrade" to the man who a few months before had been chairman of the Council of Ministers and for a long time the second most influential figure of the regime.[12] Bulganin was called upon to recant, to confess his part in the activities of the antiparty group which in 1957 had challenged Khrushchev's leadership, and to pledge his loyalty and willingness to work for the party and the state in whatever humble position was entrusted to him. Equally a part of the ritual, the assembly greeted him in silence, and some of the succeeding speakers found this declaration of a now broken man lacking in candor and completeness. Thus, amidst sullen hostility and vilification the erstwhile colleague and apparent friend of Khrushchev countersigned his own political death warrant. It fell to him to provide these unflattering portraits of his alleged partners in crime: "Molotov—a man who has lost contact with life and the Soviet nation . . . Kaganovich—an empty phrase-maker . . . Malenkov—an intriguer capable of any baseness." [13]

It is a bold man who would speak with confidence about what actually happened in June 1957. From the official Soviet version unreels a veritable serial story. In June Malenkov,

Molotov, and Kaganovich—and Shepilov, "who has jumped over to their side," as the official version stoutly and somewhat incomprehensibly insists—are publicly stigmatized and ejected from their high positions. In December the cast is increased by Bulganin. And in January 1959 at the Twenty-First Congress, Saburov and Pervukhin are officially stamped as having been involved in the antiparty attempt, though not to the extent alleged about the other five.[14] The recent party history, in describing the fracas of June 1957, implies very strongly that old Voroshilov, if not on the side of Khrushchev's opponents, at least did not oppose them.[15] The penalties meted out have also varied. The "Three Musketeers" of the opposition and their unfortunate "recruit," Shepilov, were dismissed to unimportant posts and became the targets of recurrent abuse. Bulganin, a year later, was consigned to the same category. Pervukhin was retained in the highest governing bodies of the party, though demoted to an alternate member of the Presidium and sent off to a diplomatic post. Saburov, once the head of all economic planning, is now a director of a factory. Voroshilov, probably in view of his age (b. 1881) and a certain sentimental popularity which surrounds his name, has been retained in his party and state posts, but deprived of any real influence (see my last chapter, however).

Just enough of the story is known to lead one to the most tantalizing reconstructions of intrigues and clashes at the highest levels of power. Out of insufficient data tales have been spun of the "Stalinist bloc" of Molotov, Malenkov, and Kaganovich, and the "industrial" or "managers" party represented by Pervukhin and Saburov, collaborating to unseat Khrushchev. We have already seen how in the case of agricultural policy the ruling faction managed to affix to Malenkov and Molotov the responsibility for the ruinous policy which as a matter of fact had rested on the shoulders of the then leadership of the party as a whole. Similarly, in the case of the events of June

1957, we must not accept uncritically the official version or build upon it without caution.

Why the long delay in uncovering the part allegedly played by Bulganin? Why the differential treatment applied to Saburov and Pervukhin? Possibly in June 1957 Khrushchev did not care to avow publicly how widespread the opposition to him had been and that the majority of the Presidium had been ranged against him. Possibly he was following one of the traditional techniques of the Soviet purge, that of a gradual rather than an abrupt demotion of political opponents, with the charges against them growing louder as their power and stature decreased. But another possibility deserves to be mentioned.

One of the supporters of Khrushchev at the June 1957 plenary meeting of the Central Committee was the Minister of Defense, Marshal Zhukov. He was rewarded by being made a full member of the reorganized Presidium, the first time in Soviet history that a man primarily a soldier reached that position. Three months later Zhukov was abruptly deprived of his ministry and his party posts. His sins? "Zhukov . . . [tried] to liquidate the leadership and control of the armed forces by the Party . . . In the Soviet Army with the personal participation of Zhukov there began to be propagated the cult of his personality . . ." [16] Zhukov's successor as Defense Minister, Marshal Malinovsky, referred jocularly to the whole incident as a "box on the ear" administered to this "would-be Bonaparte." [17] While the party gatherings and documents are full of references to the antiparty group and their growing list of misdemeanors, Zhukov's dereliction is passed over quickly as simply a product of the megalomania of one man, unassisted by anybody else of importance, certainly by no party figure, and something which grew and became obvious in the space of three months. In June 1957, Zhukov was a leading and rewarded collaborator of Khrushchev whose role during the war and subsequent slights at the hand of Stalin had been advertised by the party (for instance, in Khrushchev's secret speech at the Twentieth Congress); by October, he had become a discredited megalomaniac who in a puerile fashion had sought to challenge the united authority of the party and the state. The story is one of political naiveté, which under the conditions of Soviet politics not even a gallant soldier is likely to exhibit. It served the regime's purpose to present the trouble in the army as the result of the personal aberration of one man unconnected with any deeper political or social issue, just as the opposition in the *party* was reduced to an alleged nostalgia for Stalinism exhibited by a few former leaders who had lost "contact with life." Yet the realities of political life in the Soviet Union are such that no attempt to secure a degree of autonomy—whether by the army, the state, or the industrial bureaucracy—is likely to be made by a man in possession of his senses unless he has received some encouragement or support from party circles. Bulganin at one time had been Minister of Defense. During the war and after Stalin's death, he had worked closely with Zhukov. The obscure references during both the December plenum and the January congress to the effect that the erstwhile Prime Minister was "dissatisfied with his position in the Party," and the statement in the party history that even following the events of June 1957 he continued to intrigue (with whom and about what?), may well refer to his connection with Marshal Zhukov.

Of more fundamental interest than its mystery-thriller aspects is the shifting character of Soviet politics. Before addressing ourselves to this matter, it is well to set the problem in perspective.

Until a few years ago, most of the foreign (non-Communist) commentators on Soviet affairs viewed the USSR as a well-nigh perfect totalitarian structure. The perfection of the instruments of oppression, the ubiquity and intensity of the Communist propaganda, and the Soviet citizen's isolation from anything his rulers deemed undesirable for him had persuaded many that a system like this was almost invulnerable to decay or to any conceivable internal opposition (indeed, internal opposition was practically inconceivable). The only possibility of alteration was seen in the eventuality of dissension among the wielders of the instruments of power following Stalin's death, or in an external event like war. Even the few dissenting voices—such as Kennan's—sought the key to a possible change in the Soviet system in the *rulers'* growing more enlightened and realistic, less inclined to keep their people in oppression and isolation.

Some years have passed and, in response to the post-Stalin development, many writers on Soviet affairs have shifted their focus of analysis. We no longer conjecture about the party apparatus struggling with the security forces or the army for control of the whole totalitarian structure. The "forces of history" have reappeared, and many an analyst will talk of the rise of the managerial class, or of the improving standard of living and education of the Soviet citizen, and how this modifies the structure that was once assumed to be cast iron and insusceptible to change.

It is almost superfluous to insist that *both* elements must be present in our conjectures about the present state and the future of the Soviet system. Stalin's death did not *make* the USSR malleable to social and economic pressures. But by removing the one man whom the most severe economic crisis or popular dissatisfaction could not have dislodged from the pinnacle of power, it did *reveal* the intensity and complexity of social and ideological issues confronting the regime. The crisis in Soviet agriculture was most acute during Stalin's last years, but the existence of the crisis or its resolution one way or another could not affect the despot's position, though it might spell favor or disgrace for one of his lieutenants. Following Stalin's death, it became crucial for whoever aspired to supreme power that *his* agricultural policy should be popular or yield quick improvements, and that former errors and exactions in that field should be ascribed to his opponents. What swung the scales in favor of Khrushchev in June 1957 when the majority of his colleagues in the Presidium were arrayed against him? His strength in the party apparatus and skill at personal maneuverings? Certainly. But an important part must have been played by the policies with which the victorious leader managed to identify himself. A policy of economic decentralization, though this decentralization takes place mainly at the administrative rather than the decision-making level, cannot but appeal to the local party bosses who compose the majority of the Central Committee. The party secretary of Belorussia, for instance, becomes a person of greater consequence in controlling the economic life of his republic, even if the basic plans and decisions are still made in Moscow. But there are also policies which because of their general popularity are likely to invest their exponent with added strength within the party. How attractive it must be to the Soviet citizen to be told that the competition with the United States is to apply not only to the heavy producer goods which he cannot eat or use, but also to the production of butter, milk, and meat! How considerably easier must appear the task of a party functionary if, in addition to prodding the population to further efforts and sacrifices, he can point to the tangible measures the regime is taking to improve its citizens' daily life!

But it is the last example which reminds us of the, at present, unavoidable limits of the sequence: popular policies equals power within the party. Superficially Khrushchev's gambit bears a resemblance to some of the policies associated with Malenkov's ascendance. When he was being discharged in February 1955 as Prime Minister, the gravest of the charges against Malenkov consisted of his alleged un-Leninist encouragement of the production of consumer goods to the detriment of continued expansion of Soviet heavy industry. What other elements contributed to Malenkov's disgrace (then only partial) we can merely speculate about: personal feelings of the party bigwigs against the man who had been Stalin's chief lieutenant during his last years, and probably his intended successor; Malenkov's weakness in the party apparatus from which he had been removed as the price for his premiership on the morrow of Stalin's death; and so forth. But the official statement did not hesitate to ascribe the demotion to his espousal of what on the face of it must have been a popular policy with the "masses." And so Khrushchev's maneuvering, his "platform" of better living conditions for the people and a détente with the West, can in no sense be interpreted as a bowing to popular pressures; rather, it is a clever politician's gambit, supplementing his administrative maneuverings with a timely, common-sense, and popular policy. If and when the political game in Russia begins to consist *mainly* of a contest for popularity, the system will have changed far beyond its present form.

III

Soviet totalitarianism disposes of a dazzling array of instruments of compulsion and indoctrination. At the same time, it does not take much historical insight to perceive in the USSR those social pressures toward a higher standard of living, toward a modicum of security against an arbitrary act of the state, and toward professional autonomy which are characteristic of any modernized society. In contemplating this twofold aspect of Soviet politics, a Western observer, remembering how often in Soviet—indeed, in Russian—history periods of liberalization and reform have been followed by a renewed wave of centralization and oppression, may somberly forecast the triumph of totalitarianism; or he may hopefully anticipate that social forces will modify the regime to the point where, though not democracy, at least the basic social and institutional prerequisites of democracy become perceptible.

The dilemma brings to mind a similar perplexing problem in historical prognostication. Karl Marx in the middle of the nineteenth century postulated the inevitable development of capitalism toward greater and greater monopolistic concentration, on one hand, and toward greater and greater impoverishment of the working masses, on the other. Half a century later, faced with the palpable nonfulfillment of that prophecy, some German Marxists developed an ingenious interpretation in order to reconcile Marxism with economic reality. While the *natural* tendency of capitalism is toward ever-sharpening economic crises and lowered standards for the workers, the *countertendency* both in the sense of conscious measures taken by the capitalists and of self-defense by the working class does in effect contribute to a temporary frustration of Marx's prophecy without invalidating the basic Marxist analysis. This interpretation has often been held, and with reason, to be a piece of sophistry and obfuscation. And yet it was not entirely so, and the example may help us to understand the problem of forecasting the future evolution of the Soviet system.

If modern history teaches anything, it is that industrialization and modernization have definite political effects. Granted a certain level of education, the satisfaction of basic economic needs of a society brings with it the demand for, at least, rudimentary political rights and protection against arbitrary acts of the state. Not far behind lie the equally "natural" demands of professional groups for a modicum of autonomy within their sphere: the intellectuals' for freedom in intellectual pursuits, the workers' for a real autonomy of trade unions and bargaining, and so forth. An industrialized and modernized society is likely to develop a certain gloss of agnosticism not only in religious but in ideological matters. The "natural" process in the case of the USSR must be one of erosion of totalitarianism—not necessarily, as is sometimes assumed, because the people become dissatisfied or are horrified by revelations about Stalinism, but mainly because of the logic of the people's everyday pursuits and economic functions. Not through revolts, demonstrations, or even conscious dissatisfaction, but because of the changing social, economic, and cultural environment is the Soviet system being pushed away from totalitarianism.

But before we adopt a kind of democratic determinism and talk glibly of the Soviet Union's having entered upon the road toward parliamentarianism and the rule of law, it is well to consider the countertendency. This is the very clear determination of the leaders of the Soviet system not to abandon their totalitarian controls in any appreciable degree and to divert the social and political aspirations of their people toward aims and pursuits which enhance rather than threaten their power. They are not blind to the social ferment within their society and are sophisticated enough to realize the concrete if distant danger it poses for Communist totalitarianism. But they are confident that they can handle the problem. Khrushchev has said:

The theorists of social democracy and the revisionists blacken [our real] socialist democracy. According to them, "democratization" ought to mean under socialism the abdication of the leading role of the working class and *its party*, and a *return* to the forms of bourgeois democracy. If you don't have that, then in their opinion you have neither democracy nor socialism. For them, democracy is the opportunity for dazzling parliamentary speeches, for playing with combinations between parties, for advertising the flowery formula of "free elections," behind which hides the omnipotence of capital and impotence of the working class . . .[18]

How ephemeral are those fruits of democracy when compared with the real facts of democratization of life in the USSR and the passing of the functions of the state to society! With apparent seriousness, Khrushchev cites the case of sports and physical culture, which the state is ready to turn over to social organizations, and of citizen courts, which are to deal with minor cases of social misdemeanors. But lest wrong implications be drawn from this impressive account of the withering away of the state, he adds, "It is clear in itself that the transfer of some functions from organs of the state to social organizations does not at all mean the weakening of the role of the socialist state in the building of communism." [19]

Now it is easy to discern unconscious humor in Khrushchev's words, or something else again when he states, not once but twice, that there are now no cases of Soviet citizens on trial or in prison for political crimes. But it would be a mistake to see simply hypocrisy or incredible self-deception in Khrushchev's lengthy disquisition on socialism in Russia entering the stage of communism. Those are words of a man conscious of the existence of social and economic pressures and grievances in the population, and of the need of anticipating and harnessing them to the aims of the party rather than merely suppressing them. And if the average Soviet citizen is not likely to be impressed by the abolition of a state committee on sports, or the fact that a bothersome drunkard is to be judged by a court of "comrades" rather than a state court, it does not follow that Khrushchev's declamation is entirely naive or obsolete. For though the passages dealing with the transition from socialism to communism in the USSR are often ludicrous, the total effect of the appraisal of the current position and prospects of the Communist camp and of the ideas of Marxism-Leninism can hardly fail to be impressive. Who, not only among his hearers but abroad, would laughingly dismiss his proud account of the enormous growth of Communist strength since the war? Who would take as an empty boast that "the relationship of real strength in the world today is such that we will know how to throw back any aggression of any enemy?" [20] The inanities about the transition from socialism to communism and about the Soviet state visibly withering away do not sound nearly so absurd when coupled with the startlingly realistic account of the strength of the Soviet camp, of the growing power of Soviet economy and technology, and of the weakening position of the West.

It becomes clearer how the rulers propose to resolve the paradox of the retention of their totalitarian power over an industrialized and literate society. They stake that power on the revival of the doctrine and of the party which is its embodiment; on linking the progress and successes of the Soviet Union with Marxism-Leninism and the Communist Party. The arsenal of totalitarianism, its instruments of suppression, terror, and censorship are to be kept in readiness, but are to be used more sparingly while the regime bases its policies of the moment on its ability to persuade and demonstrate to Soviet citizens that Communism is a viable and vigorous way of life which has nothing to learn from or finds nothing to envy in the obsolete democratic and liberal ideas. How chimerical are the alleged blessings of parliamentary democracy compared with the Soviet achievements in space! And the fact that one third of mankind now lives under Communism is to compensate the Soviet citizen for his lack of liberty; or, rather, he is told that he already enjoys greater freedom than his British or American counterpart. Politicians no more than advertising men are likely to be unduly depressed by a non-sequitur in their formulas or slogans. Rather they see the problem as one of a continuing need for dramatic improvisations and stunts. One should not, therefore, expect Khrushchev and his colleagues to admit even to themselves that the harnessing of nuclear energy and space exploration by Russia are not necessarily connected with the monopoly of power exercised by the Communist Party; one should not await the day when by reading social and economic statistics the rulers of the USSR will become persuaded to surrender the vast powers of coercion and suppression which still remain in their hands. Quite likely, in their minds there is no contradiction between what they regard as the democratization of life in Russia and the continuation of their absolute powers.

To use a historical simile, Khrushchev's era has meant the introduction of enlightened totalitarianism in the USSR and a conscious effort to dispense with the pathological, uneconomic, and plainly unnecessary aspects of totalitarianism inherited from Stalin.

Can the regime pursue its chosen path for long without reverting to terror and isolation from the West, or stumbling into a situation where its totalitarian powers would in effect be threatened? It is instructive to see an example of the variety of political resources of which the Communist system disposes and that enable it to avoid those two extremes which foreign commentators with their fine sense of logic take to be the imminent choices before Khrushchev. The meeting of the Central Committee which concluded 1959 bore witness to the very serious troubles which Soviet agriculture had encountered during the past year. In addition to a drought, complex economic and social factors affected adversely the farm output. Criticisms addressed to the party organization in Kazakhstan, censure applied to its secretary, one of Khrushchev's closest collaborators, Belyayev, may illuminate the earlier apprehensions about the hastiness and economic feasibility of the reclamation of the virgin lands. But the year 1959 was also the year of Soviet triumphs in space exploration, and above all it was the year when Soviet foreign policy succeeded in achieving agreement on a summit meeting. And the dictator's personal triumph in being invited to the United States, of being able, paradoxically because of Soviet pushfulness on the Berlin issue, to identify himself with international conciliation and peaceful settlement, has gone far in strengthening his position, notwithstanding serious trouble on the agricultural front. This is not meant to suggest that there is a cause-and-effect relationship between troubles on the domestic front and Soviet aggressiveness in foreign policy. But the example is instructive in showing the multiplicity of devices at the disposal of the regime, devices which can divert or block the social and economic forces impinging upon its totalitarian powers, forces which may also affect the position of the leader and his entourage.

"Enemies of communism claim that the growth of culture in the Soviet Union will press for change in its social system, that the Soviet people will not [long] suffer the present system. They [the enemies of communism] do not understand what real freedom for the worker, for the people, is! The champions of capitalism represent the capitalist world as . . . the world of freedom," said Khrushchev at the December 1959 plenum.[21] And this illustrates both the Soviet leaders' awareness of the problem and their confidence, though not untinged with apprehension, that the challenge can be met. How pathetic and yet how meaningful the attempt to give the Soviet people the surrogate of democratic feeling about this meeting of bureaucrats reporting to their boss, as if it were a free meeting of a deliberative body. The story conveyed by Khrushchev to illustrate Soviet democracy again strikes one as a mixture of make-believe and sincerity, confidence and vague apprehension, so typical of his policies: the chairman of a collective farm has been promoted by the regional party secretary to a more responsible position, but the peasants of the chairman's kolkhoz beg the satrap ineffectually not to deprive them of their leader, of whom they have grown fond. And now Khrushchev "asks" his subordinate to reconsider, to accede to the masses' desire and to keep the good man on the farm. This pleasant story, which with a few changed titles and circumstances has been told about every autocracy from Harun al-Rashid's to tsarist Russia's, is intended to illustrate the extent of real democracy in the USSR.

And the make-believe democratic paraphernalia of the

oligarchs' meeting cannot conceal the resolution to solve the most pressing internal problem of Soviet Communism through a feat of social engineering enforced by the state. The problems of the peasant and the agricultural lag and of the vestiges of private enterprise and spirit inherent in the collective-farm economy are still with the Soviet rulers. One of Khrushchev's chief lieutenants has mentioned possible solutions in terms similar to those policies which have been repudiated and condemned since 1953: amalgamation of the collective farms into still huger units; equalizing of the collective farmers' incomes; and further limitation, if not extinction, of the private plot.[22] Shades of the abuses condemned by Khrushchev in 1953 and 1958 and so convincingly attributed to Malenkov and Molotov! In his own speech the dictator urged, for the present, a more cautious approach: the education of the peasant so that he will grow to like living in an apartment house and becoming a rural wage earner with no sense of ownership of his land. And so, better than long historical and philosophical disquisitions, the dialectic of Soviet agricultural policies reveals the real problem of totalitarianism in its groping to retain mastery over a changing society.

5 NATIONALISM, PANSLAVISM, COMMUNISM

The theme of continuity has been sounded with monotonous regularity in most of the discussions of the "spirit" of Russian history. The title of this essay suggests another variant on the theme. Communism, a materialistic and rationalist philosophy with international roots and pretensions, appears today to many as just another emanation of Russian imperialism of the nineteenth century, of nationalism and Panslavism founded, among other things, upon a semimystical if not obscurantist notion of the uniqueness of Russian society and the special historical mission of the Slavs.

Certainly historical parallels are striking. Stalin's Russia in 1945 realized the most extravagant dreams of the Panslavists by becoming the master of all the Slavic nations as well as of Hungary, Rumania, and Albania. In the propaganda justifying the Yalta decision to shift the frontiers of Poland westward deep into ethnically Germanic areas, the Soviet press used word for word the arguments of the nineteenth-century Panslavists and nationalists. It was Katkov who, during the Polish

SOURCE: First published in *Russian Foreign Policy: Essays in Historical Perspective*, Ivo Lederer, ed. (Yale University Press, New Haven, 1962).

rebellion of 1863, accused the historic Polish state of having betrayed Slavdom: its kings and landlords had abandoned their Slav brothers of Silesia and Pomerania to Germany and assimilation, while wresting huge territories from their Russian neighbors. Now the Georgian despot had reunited all the Ukrainians and Belorussians with their Great Russian brothers while pushing the frontiers of Germandom back to their thirteenth-century limits. Even more characteristically and paradoxically, the Soviet state presided over the removal of an age-old grievance of the Orthodox Church: helped by the secret police, the Greek Catholic Uniates of Galicia returned to the bosom of Orthodoxy.

Examples and parallels abound. What was the post–World War II campaign against cosmopolitanism, with its exaltation of the native Russian genius, but an apparent echo of Slavophilism, that twin brother of Panslavism? And if the state founded upon the philosophy of Karl Marx could not quite adopt the motto of the Black Hundreds, "Beat the Jews and save Russia," then the wave of less ostentatious but undoubtedly officially sponsored anti-Semitism of Stalin's last year provides another link between Bolshevism and the extreme nationalism of prerevolutionary Russia.

The theme of continuity is a seductive one. It has led some of the most distinguished chroniclers of Russian thought and development to lapse into a kind of Slavophilism of their own: Russia is unique among all other nations insofar as the revolutions and reformations of its modern history have been more apparent than real. The title of a study by Jan Kucharzewski, *From the White to Red Tsardom,* and the tone and conclusion of Sir John Maynard's *Russia in Flux* provide good examples in point. In less scholarly hands the theme of continuity reverts to complete obscurantism: "the Russian soul" and the "Tatar" make their scheduled appearance and provide all the answers.

It is instructive to turn to obscurantism of the opposite

variety. For all his nationalistic effusions, the Soviet historian is held severely to the Marxian scheme of social and political development. Economic and social transformations bring their political results without any mystical interventions by the *sobornost*, the Russian spirit. The story of material developments and of brave and resourceful people who, armed with a scientific theory of society, brought about the revolution and liberation of the toiling masses is as simple-minded in its utter disregard of the cultural and historical complexities of the nation as the opposite theory is in slighting the political and economic factor.

I

If a corrective is required to both the overly mechanistic and the overly emotional views of Russian history, it is easily found in an unbiased survey of Russia's role on the international scene during the past century. Personalities, ideologies, and sheer accidents have played their part alongside the economic forces and general tendencies of European politics. All during this period, tsarist and Soviet policies have enjoyed the advantage or disadvantage, depending on one's point of view, of foreign policy conducted without the *direct* interference or influence of what we call public opinion. If this statement has to be qualified when we speak of Alexander II's reign, or of the period of Russian semiconstitutionalism of 1906–1917, if it may have to be reappraised when we discuss the most recent period of Soviet foreign policy, it still remains an overwhelming fact when we compare Russia with the other great powers of the last century. The tsar's relations with foreign states were the function of a few people, ultimately the decision of the autocrat himself. Nothing entitles us to think that under Soviet conditions the deliberative process extended to a larger group than the Central Committee or since the middle twenties the Politburo-Presidium, or that at the height of *Communist* autocracy the decisions reached were not the product of one man's will. The continuous existence of dictatorship and personal rule has always made Russian policies difficult for someone immersed in Western political habits and practices to understand. The most astute Western observers have professed to see but enigmas and puzzles when it came to Russia's behavior on the international scene. Where is the main puzzle?

Part of the answer lies in the undoubted fact that in a totalitarian or authoritarian system foreign policy is much more intimately connected with internal politics than is the case in democratic and constitutional societies. Thus some of the most crucial shifts and puzzling decisions of the Soviet leaders make sense only if we keep in mind the internal conditions that accompanied them. Was Stalin's pact with Hitler an act of shortsighted duplicity and desire for territorial expansion at the cost of Poland and the Baltic states? But the despot must have also feared the probable consequences of Russia's participation in any war—even a war Russia would have fought as part of a victorious coalition—for a regime weakened by a decade of forced collectivization and purges. The same element of totalitarian prudence, almost incomprehensible to the Western mind, accounts for the abrupt isolation of the USSR following the war, when the regime brutally and needlessly (said foreign observers) dissipated the good will it had accumulated in the West, not only by its actions but also by its statements and absolute isolation from its recent allies. A slower rate of subjugation of the satellites, a friendlier tone, could have meant credits for Russia's devastated economy and a delay in the awakening of the West to the danger of Communism. But what would have been the *internal* consequences of continued intercourse and friendly relations with the West in a society that had to be spurred to even greater sacrifices on behalf of industrialization, in a nation that had been taught to expect an easier and freer life as a reward for its wartime struggle?

This leitmotif of Russia's relations with the outside world has a long history and is but awkwardly summarized by a Marxist term: uneven development. To a Russian historian in the nineteenth century, this problem appeared in categories not entirely dissimilar to the considerations that must have agitated Stalin in 1945 or Nikita Khrushchev during the "thaw." S. M. Soloviev saw something providential in Russia's defeats in the West during the last quarter of the sixteenth century: "The withdrawal of the Russian nation into the remote northeast was important because it enabled the Russian state to grow strong far from Western influences. We see that those Slav nations which have prematurely come into contact with the West, strong in its civilization and in its Roman heritage, have declined, have lost their independence and some of them even their nationhood." But the departure of Russia from Europe had also its baneful influences: backwardness and weakness of social and economic development. So, Soloviev concludes, the Russian state had to turn west again, but this time its entrance was that of a great power.[1]

To the Western mind there is something irresistibly tragicomic in the continuity that extends from Ivan the Terrible chastising Kurbsky for being impressed with Western (Polish) customs and liberties to Khrushchev's propagandists chastising Soviet youths for playing rock-and-roll records. But the serious side of the ambivalence toward what was called the West and is now branded the capitalist world has always been found in two very prosaic facts: the need of imperial authoritarianism and then of Communist totalitarianism to absorb elements of Western material culture and technology without at the same time suffering political infection from abroad, and the psychological need of the educated classes either to rebel against or to rationalize their lack of freedom and the social backwardness of their country.

Both Panslavism and Slavophilism have been attributed to

the influence of European romanticism and the ideas of Hegel and Herder permeating post-1815 Russia.[2] But it is easy to see them as a much more general phenomenon that almost always accompanies the reaction of a cultural elite of a nation to the challenge of a new, and in some respects superior, culture. We see somewhat similar symptoms in the newly arising states of Asia and Africa. Alongside the extreme eagerness to adopt Western technology and comforts, we find an almost pathetic attempt to assert the superiority of *their* cultural traditions and to respond with militant nationalism to the facts of backwardness and unpreparedness for democratic institutions. Or a parallel might even be drawn to the Southern argument in the debate between the South and North before the American Civil War: the Southern "patriarchal" institutions, for all their apparent offense to democracy, are somehow purer and of a higher order than Northern "wagery" and impersonal capitalism.

Seen in this light, the nationalist tradition in Russia, with its subcurrents of Slavophilism and Panslavism, is but the reverse side of the revolutionary tradition beginning with the Decembrists. Indeed, the arguments and emotional tone of the two are often interchangeable. A representative of the most extreme form of Russian nationalism, the protofascist Union of the Russian People, wrote before World War I: "In all the Western states which have a representative form of government there is a numerous and exacting bourgeoisie which lies like a heavy burden upon the state . . . All the Western governments . . . are based upon the bourgeoisie." [3] This analysis is hardly different from that of a Marxist or a socialist-revolutionary, characteristic of both streams of Russian radicalism which, no matter how critical of the status quo in Russia, would still proudly contrast "our" inherent superiority with "their" soulless materialism and hypocrisy. And, to be sure, the same note is not missing in the most recent utterances of Communism.

The mechanism of compensation for backwardness includes as its first consequence nationalism and, as its second, imperialism. The effusions of the Panslavists had to pass very soon beyond the general interest in Slavic cultures and languages and into the active sponsorship of unification of the Slav world under Russian leadership. Sympathy for and interest in Orthodoxy soon had to add the insistent demand that the Third Rome should recover the Second or, in prosaic terms, the demand for an annexation of Constantinople and the Straits.

Quite a few of the revolutionaries, opposed in principle to the national and political oppression of the old empire, conceived of their revolutionary activity in expansionist terms: through a revolution, backward Russia would become at once the most socially advanced state in Europe and would give the world an example and an incentive toward real democracy and republicanism, unblemished by capitalism and degenerate parliamentarianism. This spiritual and political xenophobia and intermittent anti-Westernism are thus another link in the two great radical traditions in Russia which have found their culmination in Communism.

It is beyond this point, however, that parallels cease to be valid and that Communism, not only in theory but as it has been practiced in Russia, appears as a movement and ideology quite apart from traditional Russian nationalism or Panslavism. The Communists are not and never were *simply* Russian nationalists and imperialists in Marxist clothes. Marxism in its very conception demonstrated its amazing assimilating potential: it absorbed pro-industrial liberalism and anti-industrial anarchism, fashioning out of those discordant parts a doctrine both revolutionary and deterministic. With the same assimilating capacity, the Bolsheviks have absorbed both national self-determination and Russian nationalism; they have played simultaneously the themes of internationalism and imperialism. But this capacity to absorb opposites within the same doctrine and movement can never last indefinitely. And a survey of Soviet foreign policy is most instructive in showing the growing fissures. Between 1917 and 1945 it could be believed by the Soviet leaders and Communists elsewhere, though at times it required violence to facts or persons, that the interests of Soviet or even Russian nationalism and those of the international Communist movement were in general harmony. Every increase in territory and power of the Soviet Union, every sign of the Communist regime's firmer link with its peoples, traditions, and sentiments, could be taken, no matter what Marxist orthodoxy had to say on the subject, as a gain for international Communism. Conversely, the foreign Communist parties were important assets to the Soviet state, at first its allies and cobelievers, soon its agents. But beginning with 1945 the very success of Soviet imperialism began to threaten this harmony. Communism in power, as Titoism has demonstrated, began to differentiate between its allegiance to the ideology and its obedience to the USSR. The Communist bloc now contains another great power, China, and it can never again be the monolith it had aspired to be and largely succeeded in being up to Stalin's death.

This sketch of the similarities and differences in the three creeds named in my title suggests another parallel between the old and the new. Risking a far-fetched historical judgment, one might postulate that well into the nineteenth century the interest of autocracy coincided with the Russian national interest, if by the latter is meant creating a modern (in the eighteenth-century meaning of the term) European state, with an army and bureaucracy. After the first quarter of the nineteenth century, this coincidence ends and autocracy becomes, to use a Marxist term, a fetter on the process of modernization and transformation of society. The Bolshevik regime, during its first thirty years, had the good fortune of at least making it appear plausible that the logic of industrialization and modernization of Russia (its national interest as defined in twentieth-century terms) went along with the logic of Communism and with the interest of the world proletariat. Modernization and industrialization have created social pressures the regime cannot ignore, but which it cannot fully satisfy without altering its totalitarian character. And the existence of Communist China has meant that further expansion of Communism will not always and automatically rebound to the influence and power of Moscow.

II

Nationalism is a volatile phenomenon that requires relatively modern means of communication and some degree of national literacy if it is to be a social force and not a fad sponsored by a few intellectuals or a simple xenophobic reaction of a people to foreign rule and alien customs. It is instructive to compare with actual facts the theories and fantasies woven by so many historians, writers, and statesmen of tsarist Russia about nation-wide understanding and support for the foreign aims of imperial policy. Several years after the revolution, Sazonov could still write: "Neither for Emperor Nicholas II nor for me as foreign minister was there a clearer and juster task than political rebirth of the Czechs. Russian public opinion also looked at the problem in this light." [4] It is easy today to see the air of unreality and fantasy that persuaded so many figures of imperial Russia that internal problems could be sidelined by or subordinated to foreign expansion. With the beginning of the modern period of Russian politics in 1855, even the most intense waves of nationalism or Panslavism, as during the Russo-Turkish War of 1877–78 or during the first months of the First World War, constituted but brief periods of interruption in the continuous internal crisis.

The revolutions of 1905 and 1917 exposed the absence of the most vital underpinning of modern nationalism: the sense of national cohesion. In 1905 the most striking fact, from this point of view, was not the intensity of revolutionary feeling in the two capitals, but the complete collapse of authority and social and political organization in large areas of the country. After the collapse of the empire and during the civil war, it is not surprising to find national separatism among the Ukrainians or the nations of the Caucasus, but it is startling to find occasional demands for independence among the Don and Kuban Cossacks and in Siberia.

It was indeed the rigidity and unrealism of the Whites' Great Russian nationalism that became a contributory factor in their defeat. It fell to their opponents to utilize with unrivaled skill the slogans both of nationalism and of self-determination, and thus in fact to preserve most of the empire.

When in 1919 Lenin reproached some of his comrades with being Great Russian chauvinists under a Communist veneer, he was criticizing Bukharin and Pyatakov for making explicit what was implicit in his own thoughts on the subject of nationalities and nationalism. But the infant Soviet state could not afford, nor was the Communist Party yet ready either psychologically or in fact, to modify the overwhelmingly internationalist heritage of Marxism. To be sure, the doctrine itself provided no guidance on the subject of foreign policy for a socialist state. Just as it would have been inconceivable in the canon of Marxism (as distinguished from occasional dicta of Marx himself) that socialism should conquer a society overwhelmingly agricultural in its character, so it would have been ridiculous to allow that scientific socialism should come to power in an era when nationalism rather than the social question was the main feature of the international scene. The amazing synthesis of nationalism and internationalism, of viewing international relations in the formal light of diplomacy, on the one hand, and as the supranational struggle of the proletariat with capitalism and imperialism, on the other, was taught to the Bolsheviks by the best possible teacher—the instinct for survival. This was the lesson of the civil war and the following few years, the most vulnerable period of the Soviet regime.

The first few years of Soviet power embody in themselves a dialectic of approaches toward the outside world which later became elaborated into a conscious pattern of foreign policy. It is obvious that the November uprising could not have been undertaken nor carried through with success had its organizers believed that their example would not be followed elsewhere in Europe, and that for a generation Russia would remain isolated, the only Communist state in the world. This psychology—an unhesitating commitment to internationalism and the conviction that in the wake of the Russian revolution would come socialist revolutions in other countries, notably in industrialized Germany—provided the main justification for the Brest-Litovsk Treaty. Its logical result, had Germany won the war, would have been the end of the Communist regime and the establishment of Russia as a German satellite. But Lenin's argument, which carried the day, insisted that Brest-Litovsk was in effect a truce and that revolutionary forces would soon assert themselves in the West. Thus revolutionary messianism —an uncritical acceptance of the Leninist premise that imperialism as demonstrated by the war would be followed by world revolution—was a necessary factor in the psychology of the November undertaking and in the agreement to the disastrous treaty.

The antithesis to Marxian internationalism appeared in the course of the civil and Polish wars. At first for sheer expediency, but then with increasing strength, an appeal had to be made to nationalism, with the Bolsheviks representing themselves convincingly as defenders of the historic Russian lands.

It is inappropriate either to minimize or to exaggerate the

element of tactical flexibility and expediency in these policies. Even before the war, Lenin's thinking had begun to depart from the strict materialist tenets of the Marxist canon. But the revolution was carried through in the spirit of reassertion of Marxian fundamentalism and in the conviction that it was but a first step in a general European upheaval. The extreme pressures of the period 1917–1921 did not allow the Bolsheviks to reflect that they were in fact acting on two opposite premises: internationalism and nationalism; world revolution and the territorial interests of the Russian state. By 1921 the synthesis was achieved and would remain the principle of Soviet foreign policy from then on, even though foreign observers studying only a particular situation or a period continued to label the policies of the USSR as exclusively devoted either to the Russian national interest or to international Communism.

The story of Soviet foreign policy from 1917 through World War II is one of success unparalleled in the history of diplomacy. Founded upon principles directly hostile to the established international order and frankly proclaiming its hostility to the principles upon which every European government was based, the Soviet state not only avoided being crushed by the forces of the old order, but step by step it entered into normal diplomatic and commercial relations with the world of capitalism. This admission was not purchased by any repudiation of its revolutionary character, nor, despite occasional pledges to this effect, by discontinuation of its world-wide revolutionary propaganda. To realize the achievement of Soviet policy, it is well to remember how helpless Soviet Russia would have been in the twenties and thirties in the face of a real capitalist encirclement, not to mention concerted aggression.

The policy of seeking normal diplomatic relations, trade, and credits—in brief, an earlier version of "peaceful coexistence"— was dictated again by the most obvious considerations of com-

mon sense and survival. Insensibly, this pragmatism had within
a few years completely attenuated the earlier priority of the
internationalist outlook. Even before the complete subjugation
of the Comintern to Stalin's policy, the attitude of the Russian
Communists to their foreign colleagues had become quite
different from what it had been in the early days of the revolution. In 1918–19 the news of a Communist success in Bavaria
or Hungary was just as important and exhilarating as the news
of a victory over Denikin or Kolchak. After 1921, no matter
how conscientiously the Bolsheviks felt themselves a part of
the international movement, it became almost impossible for
them to remain intensely internationalist in their preoccupations and temperament. Quite apart from any shifts in ideology
or the victory of this or that faction in the party, the psychological change was somewhat similar to that which takes place
in a man whose whole life has centered on an association or a
club and who suddenly acquires a household and family. The
image of the world revolution, of a world-wide triumph of
socialism, grew distant and blurred even before it became
subordinated to the interest of the Soviet state.

The development of the Soviet philosophy of international affairs was a product of the early twenties. From then on, the same
themes appeared, with varying intensity, until the post-Stalin
period brought a need for a basic re-examination, which is still
going on. What are the themes? There is, first of all, acceptance
of the system of states and of the durability of capitalism—a
premise drastically opposite to that held by the Bolsheviks
between 1915 and 1920. When Lenin said that it would be
much more difficult for a revolution to start in the West than
in Russia and that, contrariwise, once successful, a Communist
revolution in the West would bring socialism more easily and
speedily than in his own country, he completed a reappraisal
of the fundamental tenets of Marxism which began with his
What Is To Be Done? He was formulating at the same time

the real theoretical justification of "socialism in one country."
In an industrialized country it would require a special combination of circumstances, and not just an internal deteriora-
tion of economy, to bring about Communism. A highly
industrialized country is relatively immune to revolutionary
socialism, and at times, as in the early twenties in its developed
sector, international capitalism can become stabilized. Therefore the necessity of coexistence with the capitalist world became mandatory, just as the necessity of internal development
and the security of the country that had achieved the rudiments
of socialism had to become the supreme aim of the world
proletariat and take priority over the temporary success of this
or that Communist Party.

This interpretation of Lenin's views was subsequently challenged by Trotsky in his struggle with Stalin: "To give an
integral outline of Lenin's economic and political views conditioned by the international character of the socialist revolution
would require a separate work that would cover many subjects,
but not the subject of building a self-sufficient socialist society
in one country, because Lenin did not know this subject." [5]
But in fact Trotsky's behavior up to 1923–24, when he found
himself in increasing opposition to the ruling group, reflected
this common-sense acceptance of the realities of the situation
which later on were to be called socialism in one country and
coexistence.

For what indeed could be the alternative? Could the Soviet
state enter into armed conflict with the main capitalist powers,
and that without having become an industrial power? In criticizing the draft program of the Sixth Congress of the Comintern, Trotsky attacked its statement that socialism can be built
on the basis of a national state if only there is no foreign
intervention: "From this there can and must follow (notwithstanding all pompous declarations in the draft program) a
collaborationist policy towards the foreign bourgeoisie with

the object of averting intervention, as this will guarantee the construction of socialism, that is to say, will solve the main historical question." [6] It is characteristic of the tactical ineptitude of Trotsky that he found himself forced to develop to its extreme limits a formula of internationalism that took no account of the realities of the international situation and was bound to be misunderstood and unpopular among the rank and file of the party. When at the Fifteenth Party Conference Trotsky stated that he had never doubted the *possibility* of building socialism in Russia, but only thought the task could not be *completed* while the capitalist world encircled the USSR, this subtle formula sounded like a lot of double talk to the new party officialdom which had already been won over to the simpler, apparently common-sense formulations of Stalin.[7]

The theme of socialism in one country did not mean in 1925, any more than peaceful coexistence has in recent years, a repudiation of the expansionist tendencies of Communism. The alleged ideological disagreement between Stalin and Trotsky consisted, apart from the question of power and tactics, in a conflict of two types of revolutionary temperament: one seeing the problem of Communist expansion from the angle of organization and careful preparation of the base; the other trusting in the spontaneous revolutionary enthusiasm of the masses at appropriate historical moments. There is no denying that for the purposes of intraparty struggle Trotsky made an appeal to what he imagined was internationalist sentiment, while Stalin exploited what with some stretching of the term might be called nationalism, or at least concern for the USSR. Would the policy of the Soviet regime have been drastically different had Trotsky rather than Stalin succeeded in grasping rule? Probably not, insofar as concrete policy measures were concerned, though the spirit and tone of Communist propaganda would have been different. It is impossible to believe that the German Communists might have seized power in 1923 except for the pusillanimity of their leadership and of the Comintern or that different tactics by the Chinese Communists could have destroyed Chiang Kai-shek. The main characteristic of the 1920s, whether reflected in the activity of the Comintern or of the Narkomindel, was prudent realism—the awareness of Russia's industrial and military weakness.

The other main theme of foreign policy between the revolution and Stalin's death had already been expounded in Lenin's *Imperialism:* any stabilization of capitalism is of necessity temporary. Its Götterdämmerung will come primarily as a consequence of the increased competition between the imperialist powers for investment markets, culminating in imperialist wars and the colonial nations' struggles against their masters. Theoretically, this thesis was often stated with a certain grossness and naiveté; to Trotsky it appeared probable that the two main capitalist powers, the United States and Great Britain, would sooner or later clash in sharp conflict. As late as 1952 Stalin in his *Economic Problems of Socialism* could still revert to this crude version of Lenin's thesis. But, as in many other cases, the theoretical naiveté of the Communist outlook went along with a basic insight: the economic and psychological underpinnings of the European state system had been destroyed beyond recall by the war of 1914 and then by Versailles. Neither the League of Nations nor the French system of alliances nor the new domination of the world's economy by America could restore the old pattern of international capitalism and its political consequences: the steady progress of liberal and democratic institutions. With liberalism having become impotent, the role of the main enemy to the spread of Communism had been assumed by democratic socialism. The fight against social democracy became the external expression of the struggle against "spontaneity" that went back to Lenin's *What Is To Be Done?*

The temptation to encourage the fissiparous tendencies of

the capitalist world order clashed with the recognition that a major international crisis could not only lead to further weakening or destruction of capitalism but might prematurely involve and destroy the infant Soviet state. We might characterize Soviet foreign policy between 1921 and 1939 as pacifism tempered by Communist ideology. Its major analytical premise became not so much a belief in the unlimited attractiveness of Communism as confidence in the self-destructive capacity of capitalism, and not for the reasons originally spelled out by Marx.

The two main themes of the Soviet appraisal of the world situation are best illustrated by the reaction to the world economic crisis of 1929–1934. Its coming intensified the Communist drive against the social democrats and the Stalinization of the foreign parties. In a most remarkable reassertion of the ideological component, Hitler's assumption of power was taken as part of the script: fascism was the last (brief) stage of capitalism.

Yet, at the same time, the Soviet regime experienced its greatest apprehension over foreign conflict; the theory of coexistence was stressed most vigorously; and the Soviet Union put unusual stress on the restoration of normal diplomatic relations with the United States. The period immediately preceding the policy of the popular front and the entrance into the League of Nations showed the greatest emphasis on ideology since the twenties, but even so it bore but faint resemblance to the millenarian revolutionary expectations and unhesitating internationalism of 1917–1920. It is the inevitable pragmatism which comes with power and responsibility, and not corruption as the Trotskyites would have it, which led Stalin to favor Soviet nationalism over the interests of the international proletariat.

The decade of the thirties brought what had been implicit in Stalinism since the middle twenties: the greater and greater self-identification of the regime with Russian nationalism. It was not only that the hazy slogan of capitalist encirclement gave way to the concrete and openly announced threat of Hitler's Germany. The tremendous task of social and industrial reconstruction required the mobilization of all the political and propaganda resources at the disposal of the regime. The efforts of the tsarist regime to inculcate the nationalist cult look puny and ineffective when contrasted with all the agencies and means set at the disposal of the modern totalitarian state. The evocation of Russia's past military weakness and defeats was one of the main rationalizations used by Stalin to justify the sufferings and privations of forced industrialization and collectivization. Again, it is nearsighted and erroneous to view the inculcation of patriotism and official sponsorship of bourgeois values and motivations as a departure from Marxism or as a "great retreat." The new system of values, the modification of Marxist phraseology and symbols through an admixture of patriotic and bourgeois ones, were necessary to enable the USSR to achieve something the old regime had never been given a chance to accomplish: a modern, industrialized, and centralized state.[8] It is not surprising that, among the charges preferred in the purge trials, treason and subservience to foreign governments were attributed to the alleged oppositionists alongside equally fantastic accusations of "wrecking" and class betrayal.

It seems astonishing in retrospect to think that the Russian moves in 1939–1941 should have surprised and shocked the West, or that the reasons behind the Soviet-German Pact should still remain a subject of contention. Granted the premises of Soviet foreign policy and the internal situation of the USSR in 1939, no other course of action was open to Stalin than that which was taken in precipitating World War II. The usual interpretations range from attributing Stalin's decision to his distrust of the Western Allies, because of their behavior during the Munich crisis and their dilatoriness in the military negotiations with Russia, to his desire to provoke a prolonged world conflict from which the USSR might emerge the real victor. The main consideration was quite simple: the absolute necessity of avoiding a situation in which the USSR would become militarily involved. Once before Russia had fought a war as part of a victorious coalition but this had not prevented Russian military defeat, collapse of the regime, and disintegration of the empire. It was then inconceivable that the Soviet rulers, bearing this experience in mind and conscious of the prodigious sacrifices exacted by a decade of collectivization and purges, would have risked war even if the Western powers had been most prompt and reassuring in their negotiations and even if the problem of the passage of Russian troops through Poland and the Baltic states had been settled according to Soviet demands. Alliance with the West would have meant for the USSR undoubted involvement in a shooting war with all its incalculable consequences. The treaty with Hitler meant immediate territorial gains as well as the seductive prospect of a long and indecisive war between the main capitalist powers with all its alluring social and economic consequences. More realistic than their predecessors in 1914, Russia's rulers had no illusions as to the extent of support their peoples would give them in the event of war.*

* This interpretation is subject to the following criticisms: (1) A firm Soviet commitment to the West would have in the first place prevented the war. (2) Even after their treaty with Hitler, the Russians could not have been sure that the Western Allies would not capitulate over Poland à la Munich, thus leaving them in an even more exposed position in regard to Germany than before. The first objection is disposed of by the fact that Hitler was already prepared to go to war over Sudetenland *without* a prior guarantee of Russian nonintervention. Under (2) one must simply conjecture that the Russians gauged more correctly than the Germans the degree of the Western powers' involvement on behalf of Poland. If after the destruction of the Polish state they officially seconded the German argument that there was now no reason for continuing the war, the explanation is again quite obvious: they were frightened to do or say anything out of step with the policy of their terrible allies.

The preceding discussion illustrates how indirect the influence of ideology on the policies of a totalitarian regime can be. The main factor in the decision of 1939 was not nationalism in the proper sense of the word, though as a result the Soviet Union gathered most of the territories lost in the post-World War I settlement, absorbed for the first time in Russian history the Ukrainians of Galicia, and attempted less successfully to reclaim the tsarist heritage in Finland and to realize traditional Russian aspirations in the Straits. Nor can the decision be classified as a dramatic rejection of the ideological premises of Communism. The abrupt shift did not affect the essentially Marxist-Leninist character of the analysis of the world situation by the Soviet leaders. A general European war, provided the Soviet Union were not drawn into it, would hasten the decomposition of the capitalist world and increase the opportunities for Communism in the West and elsewhere. The aspirations of nationalism and the analytical framework of Communism become simply subsumed in the interest of the totalitarian regime. Viewed in this light, the Soviet-Nazi Pact was neither more nor less a betrayal or basic shift in the foundations of Soviet policy than Rapallo or the Soviet entrance into the League of Nations.

The totalitarian Realpolitik that inspired Stalin's moves in 1939 can be best brought into relief if we compare it with Russia's entrance into World War I. A tangle of moral and treaty obligations, nationalist and Panslavist sentiments outraged by the pressure on a small Slavic country, they all combined in the decision that foredoomed the empire. Yet tsarist statesmen must have kept in mind the internal lessons of the Russo-Japanese War. The authoritarian regime found itself a captive not only of its international obligations but also of its own ideology, though both pointed in a direction which threatened the very principle of authoritarianism itself. To the moralizing historian there must be an added source of chagrin in the reflection that Stalin's almost catastrophic miscalculation was due not to the inherent wickedness of his totalitarian raison d'état, but to a common and morally neutral failing of political realism: the expectation of a modicum of rationality in the behavior of others. It must have appeared inconceivable to him in 1939 that the great Western powers would contemplate war when they were so badly prepared that their armies would eventually collapse in a few weeks before the German onslaught. In the spring of 1941 it must have been almost equally difficult to believe, despite all the abundant warnings and intelligence reports, that, with Great Britain still unconquered, Germany would attack the Soviet Union.[9] Hence Stalin rejected as a provocation all rumors and reports of German preparations for invasion.

Did the experience of the war affect the main bases of Soviet foreign policy? To a superficial observer, nationalism appears to have displaced Communism as the main ideological prop of the regime. Certainly, the dissolution of the Comintern, the use of nationalistic symbols, the abeyance of class and ideological slogans and gestures of toleration toward the Orthodox church might suggest, if one did not look deeply enough, a major reappraisal and a basic change in the Soviet system. But even before the end of hostilities, indications were not lacking that, while nationalism had been firmly absorbed into Soviet ideology, it had not replaced Marxism-Leninism.

The war did not bring a basic reorientation in Soviet foreign policy because nothing during its last stages or during the immediate postwar period affected the cardinal point of the Soviet analysis of international relations: the self-destructive tendency of the capitalist world and its utter inability to reconstruct a feasible world order.

With some modifications, the guiding principles of postwar policies remained the ones of 1921–1939. The apparently enigmatic character of Soviet behavior in the post-World War II world was caused in fact by the erratic nature of the United States response to the Soviet challenge. Looking at it from the Russian perspective, it must have appeared most illogical for the United States to concede Eastern Europe and yet to prove obstinate about the status of Berlin. Despite all the wartime lessons in the Western Allies' tractability or naiveté, it still must have loomed inconceivable in 1945 that America would ever tolerate complete subjugation of China by the Communists. Not only in their statements but by their actions the Soviets indicated that they counted on Chiang Kai-shek's remaining for a long time a major factor in the politics of mainland China.[10] It was then clearly unexpected that the Americans, having surrendered their main position in Asia, would react so violently to a tidying-up operation in Korea. Stalin's policy has often been described as warlike. Semantically speaking, this is a gross misstatement. At no point between 1945 and 1952 can it be demonstrated that the Soviet Union contemplated a major war, or that it ever undertook a course of action which by any rational criteria at the disposal of the Russians threatened to involve them in a major conflict.

It is fashionable in analyzing Soviet policies to ask about their ultimate aim, or the real inspiration: Communism or the national interest. The period 1945–1952 suggests how, paradoxically, even the posing of this question may constitute an obstacle to the understanding of Soviet foreign policy. The Soviet Union and Communism simply moved in any direction where there appeared to be a vacuum and lack of resistance. Wherever the vacuum threatened to be filled up by the interest and active support of the other great power, as in Azerbaijan in 1946 or in Turkey, aggressive policies were given up or indirect methods were substituted for direct ones. In a sense the pattern was reminiscent of the pre-1914 modus operandi of great-power diplomacy; the Soviet territorial aims were those of imperial Russia: the Balkans, northern Persia, and Manchuria.

In his celebrated analysis of Soviet foreign policy, George Kennan linked the hope for its eventual shift to the failure of its ideological assumptions about the collapse of capitalism: "For no mystical, Messianic movement—and particularly not that of the Kremlin—can face frustration indefinitely without eventually adjusting itself in one way or another to the logic of that state of affairs." [11] Quite apart from whether the Soviet Union did in fact experience a particular sense of frustration about the postwar world, the statement begs the question of the nature of Soviet ideology and its impact on the Communist appraisal of the world. Not since 1921 could the main objectives and premises of Communism be described as mystical or messianic. The visions of a self-generated collapse of capitalism and of world revolution have occupied in actual Soviet policies the same role that the vision of a world occupied exclusively by democratic and law-abiding nations obediently submitting their disputes to an international organization which renders its decisions with no consideration of power politics has occupied in the American Weltanschauung: a pleasant, exhilarating, and distant goal sincerely believed in but hardly a guide to everyday policies. In the case of Soviet policies the messianic vision has at times, as in 1930–1933, obscured the reality of the international situation, but not as often and as insistently as our own ideological goal has distorted the perspectives of allegedly pragmatic American foreign policy.

The ideological residue of Marxism in Soviet policies has indeed been quite different in character from messianism or mysticism. It has imparted to them a fairly realistic conception of the connection between economic and social forces and politics. No one brought up in the Marxist tradition could have assumed that the granting of a constitution and independence to the Congo would turn a motley of primitive communities into a constitutional democracy. The Marxist inheritance has preserved Soviet foreign policy from the "democracy—yes" type of mysticism that has characterized public opinion in the

West on so many issues. Not that the basically realistic Marxian analysis has always been free in Soviet hands from crude and oversimplified distortions; witness the Varga dispute when the official verdict forecast another capitalist depression shortly after World War II, and the anachronistic view of the capitalist world contained in Stalin's last work. But, in general, Marxism has given the Soviets an analytical framework that has served them well in their foreign policies, rather than a mystique of millenarian expectations.

It alerted them very early to the main battleground of postwar politics: the underdeveloped countries. Indeed, the whole history of Communism and of Russia must have endowed the Soviet leaders with a particular sensitivity to the problem and with an instinct for its exploitation. As early as the San Francisco meeting of the United Nations, Molotov raised in harsh tones the issue of colonialism, at the same time that the Soviet Union was entering the most brutal phase of enforcing its rule in Eastern Europe. Not in their fondest dreams could the Communists have anticipated the successes that would accrue to them in this field largely because of the blundering inconsistent and uncoordinated policies of the West. Intermittent repression often followed by capitulation, the grant of independence without having secured the most rudimentary social and economic prerequisites for a viable statehood, not to mention constitutionalism and democracy, these policies have resulted in the opening of vast new areas to Communist influence. For the purpose of harassment of the West without the risk of precipitating a major war, and of showing to their own peoples the allegedly free world to be everywhere in retreat and confusion, the African and Asian situations present the Soviet leaders with an almost embarrassingly rich choice of opportunities.

The defenders of autocratic institutions who attempted to justify them in the name of Panslavism and Slavophilism ran into insurmountable difficulties in their attempts to find an ideological prop for the oppressive social and political system. Liberal and constitutional ideas moved irresistibly throughout nineteenth-century Europe. In setting up their independent states, the Serbs and the Bulgarians did not copy the autocratic example of their Russian brothers but looked unhesitatingly for examples and lessons from England, France, and Germany. Emergent nationalism in the Asian countries sought inspiration in liberalism from Paris and London rather than St. Petersburg. The trouble with any ideological defense of the pre-1905 status quo lay in the fact of Russia's growing isolation from the political customs of the civilized world and in the unattractiveness of its system to the newly emergent states. Panslavism apart from anything else was a psychological reaction to and attempt to overcome Russia's *ideological* isolation in the nineteenth-century world. Yet as a proselytizing creed it failed even more abjectly than in other respects.

How paradoxically different is the situation today! The "inner rebel" of today can no longer gain comfort from the belief that his country is an isolated fortress of despotism that cannot for long withstand the pressures and example of the rest of the civilized world. Apart from genuine belief or indoctrination, a powerful argument for the acceptance of present Soviet reality as the best possible world can be found in recent events from Cuba to the Congo, in the inability of the Western forces to check the evanescence of their influence, and in the apparent capacity of the Soviet regime to gain support and arouse emulation even in non-Communist areas of the non-Western world. To a degree, this has become a vital part of the regime's internal propaganda. In the USSR today the official creed no longer bears any relevance to current social problems, and far-reaching modernization and industrialization have made the totalitarian framework appear increasingly unnatural. Foreign successes as well as internal reforms have enabled the regime to conceal these inherent contradictions and to prevent dissatisfaction with the present from growing into the vision of a different future. In a sense—and what a tribute to the flexibility of Communism and its leaders' ability to exploit any situation for propaganda purposes—the current argument that Soviet strength is a justification of the regime recalls the exactly reverse theme of the twenties and thirties. It was then the fact of "capitalist encirclement"—of Russia's weakness and isolation—that was used as the rationale of deprivation, the police state, and the need for sacrifices. Today it is the reality of the strength of the Soviet bloc and the apparently irresistible advance of Communism that discourage the Soviet citizen from translating his aspirations into political protest.

III

The theme of continuity, then, is misleading, if enticing. Communism has *not* turned into Russian nationalism. Like all great social creeds, Marxism-Leninism has been able to synthesize and assimilate the most diverse and apparently irreconcilable ideologies and movements. It has absorbed nationalism and at times has used the Panslavist motif. The two movements, as elaborated ideologies, were originally the product of small intellectual circles and coteries in nineteenth-century Russia. They were taken over by the tsarist regime when, as after the Crimean War, the principle of legitimacy and conservatism no longer sufficed, and a popular ideology was needed to bolster up authoritarianism. But nationalism as a viable political ideology rather than a formless sentiment needs a concrete social and political content, and the absence of this, as the example of prerevolutionary Russia suggests, makes it ineffective as an antidote to social radicalism. The Bolsheviks, we have seen, at first merely used the appeal of nationalism in their struggle for survival, but from 1921 on the needs and cares of their state took on increasing precedence over their commitment to internationalism, and this, it has been argued here, would have been true no matter which faction prevailed in the interparty struggle for power. The ability to combine Communism and nationalism reached its highest point during and immediately following World War II, but at no moment was the adoption of national and traditional symbols and slogans accompanied by the abandonment of Communist goals or of the essentially Marxist analysis of the international situation. At no point, on the other hand, did the ambition to achieve the traditional goals of the state push the Russians into rash action. The Russo-Finnish War was undertaken only when it promised to involve no military or political risks. The existence of large Ukrainian and Belorussian populations outside the borders of the USSR between 1921 and 1939 must have been viewed as a major threat to the unity of the state, but not until Poland lay prostrate did the Russians take steps to liquidate the potential Ukrainian Piedmont. Territorial aspirations to northern Persia and the Straits were not allowed to lead the USSR to the brink of an actual war.

A general survey of Soviet foreign policy indicates the soundness of its analytical framework. At the same time, it has been suggested that in the last seven or eight years the Soviet leaders have found themselves compelled to reappraise the basic premises of their policies and that this process of re-examination and searching for new formulas is still going on.

We have mentioned the amazing synthetic quality and assimilating capacity of Communism in regard to other ideologies and movements. But history teaches that this capacity of an ideology or movement can never last indefinitely. The case of liberalism is very instructive. Western liberalism in its heyday displayed the ability to absorb and contain the postulates of national self-determination and of imperialism, of free enterprise and of social reform, of political democracy and of capitalism. The English liberal of 1850 could without any feeling of inconsistency support British expansion in India as contributing to progress and civilization and sympathize with the national aspirations of the Poles and Italians. His support for the extension of the franchise did not clash with his belief in the state's noninterference in the economic field. Then in two or three decades this synthesis broke down. Political democracy was seen as a threat to liberal orthodoxy in economics. The working class, having achieved the franchise because of liberal principles, now turned against these principles. Nationalism and old-fashioned liberalism parted company. The old formula was broken and with it the magical assimilating power and the early self-confident mood of liberalism.

Like liberalism, Communism today is being threatened by its very successes. The internal aspect—the difficulty of finding a further raison d'être for Communism in the present state of Soviet society—has already been mentioned. In the wider sphere the new era was signaled by the challenge of Titoism in 1948. It was not so much the defection of a small country—heresies, apostasies, and splits are an old story in Communism—but the phenomenon it illustrated that gave warning of forthcoming trouble. The old equation, Communism equals Soviet patriotism, no longer held true in the case of *foreign* Communists who had achieved power in their own countries. The two paths have begun to diverge.

The problem was obscured during Stalin's last years, as was its domestic counterpart, by the stepping up of repression and purges. Yugoslavia remained an isolated example of dissident Communism, but by their very pressure on the remaining satellites the Russians emphasized the broader nature of the phenomenon of Titoism. In his last work Stalin showed that his thinking on international problems had not been affected by the postwar development. No mention is made of the need to elaborate a new pattern of relations for the Communist bloc. The main fact of international relations for Stalin in 1952, as it had been for the generation of the Communists he represented, was the inherent conflict within the capitalist bloc.[12] The problem of the peoples' democracies was for the despot not a major one, and it could always be resolved by tighter Soviet controls, by assimilating the economy and society in the satellites to the Soviet pattern, and by a veneer of equality and consultation between the reigning Communist parties, such as the Cominform provided.

Stalin's successors found themselves in the middle of both an international and a domestic crisis. This crisis was not brought about, as has often been assumed, by the struggle for succession to the dead tyrant or by a clash between the Stalinist and anti-Stalinist factions in the Presidium of the Central Committee. The full extent of the crisis was merely bared by the struggle for power and, while there must have been differences in attitudes toward foreign affairs, there is no reason to suppose that there was any basic disagreement among the main contenders on the necessity of liquidating the worst aspects of Stalinism in foreign as well as in domestic affairs.

Since 1953 the impact of foreign affairs on the domestic issues of Soviet politics has been more important than at any time since 1920–21. During Stalin's reign the dictator's position was never seriously affected by the fortunes of Communism abroad. Neither the defeat of the Chinese Communists in the beginning nor the defection of Yugoslavia toward the end of his reign posed a threat to the despot's power, or for that matter made much of a difference in internal Soviet politics. There is little doubt, however, that the upsets in satellite policy in 1956 had considerable internal effect. They account most probably for Khrushchev's temporary eclipse during the winter of 1956–57, and their reverberations spilled over the frontiers of the USSR and affected sections of the Soviet intelligentsia and the students. Foreign policy and foreign Communists have again become the shield of domestic dictatorship, foreign successes and the belief in the eventual triumph of Communism everywhere a major part of the rationale of totalitarianism.

It was the need to reassert ideology to demonstrate that Communism, stripped of its Stalinist excrescences, has enough historical truth and appeal to provide a viable philosophy of internal as well as international politics that dictated the domestic "thaw" and the new policies within the Communist bloc. The upsets of 1956–57 did not change this resolution, though they provided the Soviet rulers with a more realistic picture of the dangers and allowable limits of liberalization. The internal reforms have been accompanied by a campaign for an ideological revival and by the officially sponsored discussion of the further goals of Communism, a discussion which by its artificiality and nebulousness can only suggest how little is left in Marxism-Leninism to provide concrete goals for the society. The fissiparous tendencies within the Soviet bloc are likewise to be overcome by stress on the ideology. With China in the bloc, the military and industrial preponderance of the Soviet Union can no longer be the sole guarantee of its cohesion. Ideological unity is called upon to minimize and confine to the family circle the growing clash of the two great Communist powers, and to provide a veneer over what still remains the imperial rule of the Soviet Union over the satellites.

If Titoism bared one aspect of the potential clash of the interests of the Soviet Union and those of world Communism— the emergence of what has been called National Communism —then Communist China has posed a much more fundamental threat to the alleged identity of interests of world and of Soviet Communism. Yugoslavia has been an example of how non-Russian Communists once in power acquire a complex of interests and viewpoints which makes them no longer automatically responsive to the dictates of Moscow. The problem of Titoism, had there been no China, could have been solved or alleviated under the new formula the post-Stalin regime has applied in its satellite policy; the grant of internal economy, the admissibility of separate (but not too separate) roads to socialism, plus the fact of Russia's enormously greater strength might have allowed both for Russia's domination and the satellites' (that is, their Communist parties') contentment. But the emergence of China has transformed this question from one of inter-Communist diplomacy to one that goes to the very root of the basic premise of Soviet ideology and totalitarianism: do the interests of the Soviet Union benefit or suffer from a further spread of Communism and from the growth in military and industrial power of another Communist country?

To pose this question openly would mean, the Russian leaders are well aware, the beginning of the end of Soviet Communism. Furthermore, the Chinese Communists are evidently aware of this fact, and it explains why despite their infinitely weaker position they have assumed the aggressive posture in intra-Communist councils. The logic of events has imposed upon the Soviet Union the policy of coexistence with the capitalist world. The logic of their ideological commitments imposes upon the Russians the necessity of furthering Communist expansion. All around the world the decay of Western influence has left within the grasp of Communism glistening prizes to be picked up at apparently little cost, and yet at terrible risk. Like a rentier clipping off coupons, so the Russians can today gather the dividends of world-wide political trends and of the West's past policies. But this picture, the realization of the fondest dreams of the early Communists, can now cause but little real exhilaration combined as it is with the specter of nuclear war and the apprehension that Soviet foreign policy has become, for the first time, a prisoner of the ideology.

The official Soviet reaction to the dilemma has followed the maxim of a celebrated American philosopher: "Don't look behind; something might be gaining on you." To the Communists of Khrushchev's generation, it is probably psychologically impossible to formulate consciously the inherent conflict of the two lines of policy they are pursuing. (How many American statesmen would admit the possibility—indeed high probability—of a clash between the United Nations, as it is being constituted, and the basic aims of United States policy?) It is better not to look "behind," into the full logical implications of peaceful coexistence on the one hand and of a further expansion of Communism on the other. In fact, with regard to the capitalist world the Soviet Communists now advocate their own version of containment: being increasingly hemmed in and pushed on the international scene, the Western powers will suffer a gradual attrition of influence and ideology until their peaceful collapse will remove the threat of a nuclear conflagration. This premise, which must go ill with their ingrained sense of realism, is balanced by an equally wishful assumption about future intra-Communist developments: the tie of ideology and the common interest in the destruction of the capitalist world and the avoidance of nuclear war will check the fissiparous tendencies within the bloc and preserve Soviet domination. But the galling fact remains that at the height of its power and influence the Soviet state is no longer, as was the weak USSR of the twenties and thirties, the undoubted master of the Communist world and a free agent in its foreign policies.

That the dilemma is real and not just the product of wishful thinking in the non-Communist world can best be demonstrated by the behavior of the Chinese Communists during the past several years. Beginning with their encouragement of the satellite parties' autonomy vis-à-vis Moscow in 1956, through their diatribes in 1958 against revisionism and finally their much more aggressive posture toward the West, the Chinese have demonstrated a calculated intransigence toward their senior partner. Their position becomes understandable only on the premise of their fear that the Soviets might lapse into an agreement with the West, that "peaceful coexistence" might from a phrase become insensibly the correct description of Soviet foreign policy, and that support for neutralist regimes might from a tactic become a policy of unconcern for the spread of Communism in the underdeveloped areas.

History has not always justified the rationalist premise of Marxism that the observable social and political tendencies *must* work themselves out to the full. Strict logic would urge that the triad, nationalism–world Communism–totalitarianism, may no longer be confined within the same system and the same ideology. Can the magic of ideology indefinitely push away the apprehension that industrialized, modernized, and totalitarian China might become a greater threat to the national interest of the Soviet Union than the West? Can the USSR achieve a standard of living comparable to that of Western Europe while retaining unchanged its ideology and its totalitarianism? But it is possible for societies, just as it is for individuals, to go on with their basic conflicts unresolved or to seek a solution in an irrational and violent manner. Hence it is impossible to pinpoint the date when the Soviet leaders will openly face or attempt to resolve the incompatibility of the main premises of their foreign policy. All we can affirm is this paradox: at no point since the revolution and the civil war has Communist ideology been of more crucial importance to Soviet foreign policy than at present, when for the first time the national interest of the USSR and the cause of world Communism can no longer be synonymous.

6 SOCIALISM IN CURRENT SOVIET HISTORIOGRAPHY

The Soviet historian, writes the official organ, dare not be merely "a bystander, or a copyist of materials [or] a collector of evidence which by chance has fallen into his hand." [1] He is an active participant in the work of socialist construction, an exponent of Marxism-Leninism, an interpreter of the past in the light of guidance laid down by his party and the state. An exasperated Western observer may feel, after having absorbed a quota of contemporary Soviet historiography, that the art of writing modern history in the USSR has come to resemble that of an American writer on etiquette. The problem of what to do with the bride's divorced father who shows up at the wedding typifies the major methodological and classificatory dilemmas involved in assigning a "correct" place in history to, say, Plekhanov. The father of Russian Marxism cannot be assigned the place of honor because of the transgressions of his later days, nor can he be pushed out of the church because of

SOURCE: Originally written for the Conference on Contemporary History in the Soviet Mirror, held in Geneva, July 1961, under the joint auspices of *Survey*, L'Institut Universitaire des Hautes Etudes Internationales, and the Congress for Cultural Freedom.

his organic connection with the proceedings. Exactly *where* to put him in the church and what degree of reverence and cordiality to observe toward him are the questions which confront a conscientious Soviet historian; and his answers, like those of Emily Post, have to be precise and in complete agreement with the accepted theory and practice.

Yet it would be a mistake to allow this unfortunate aspect of Soviet historical writing to obscure its significance or to produce a feeling of condescension toward the Soviet historian. The latter works under a variety of pressures and compulsions which can hardly be fully appreciated outside the USSR. And their relative absence in the West has not led to a great flowering of the social sciences or a freedom from fads and timidity. The allowable limits of historical criticism in Russia are never extended to the point where the writer can give full rein to his scholarly and critical propensities. It is precisely the periods of liberalization, the "thaws," which confront him with the greatest danger. The ukase which ended the period of freer historical writing following the Twentieth Party Congress was emphatic and characteristic in its philosophy: "In the review by Yevsarov and in a number of other pronouncements, the editorial board has called for an objective appraisal of even such figures as Lassalle and Bakunin. What was it if not a call for a revision of their appraisal which had been given by Marx, Engels, and Lenin?" [2] In a sense, the historian's dilemma reflects the general one of Soviet society: life and social forces grow and change and they press upon the framework laid down by totalitarianism. The regime seeks to reconcile dogma and life, but it balks and resorts to repression each time that this liberalization encroaches upon a fundamental matter of belief. The historian's picture of the past, just as the writer's of the present, now has to be convincing as well as orthodox.

I

The problem of socialism is for the Soviet historian the central one of modern history, just as it is the most delicate one to deal with. The basic premise of the successors of Stalin has been that the diminution of physical repression would be compensated for by a revival and a reactivation of ideology. Communism was no longer to be something to be learned by rote, but a vigorous and victorious creed not afraid to reveal its antecedents and expose its errors. Other branches of socialism were not necessarily to be exhibited as heresies, and their exponents were not always presented as renegades. The task of the historian was to project this proselytizing picture of Communism into the past, to rescue the creed from the Byzantine stiffness of Stalinism, and to endow it with a humanitarian and catholic gloss. While the Soviet leaders took to visiting Belgrade and New Delhi, their academic subordinates were called upon to visit Plekhanov, Proudhon, and young Marx.

The signal was given in an editorial from *Voprosy istorii* in March 1955. Here Soviet historians were called upon to study the early history of socialism in Russia, to expand their studies of men like Belinsky and Herzen beyond the usual classificatory determination as early specimens of "bourgeois-democratic" liberalism. The neglect of socialist thought in the Fatherland of Socialism was revealed in the statement that only two universities (Moscow and Odessa) had been offering full courses in the history of socialist thought.[3] Utopian socialism, it was pointed out, was a proper field for research, since it had been a necessary prologue to the development of scientific socialism and not merely an obscurantist perversion.

The new era, which was to end abruptly in March 1957, was connected of course with the condemnation of the cult of per-

sonality. But the change was envisaged to go beyond the removal of the litany to Stalin with which for a generation before
1954 every Russian historian, just as every writer in the Soviet
Union, had to open and conclude his work. Communist historiography, like every branch of party-controlled intellectual
endeavor, had begun to suffer from monotony, lack of élan, and
sheer implausibility. Party history under Stalinism ceased to
be merely tendentious and propagandistic and became ludicrous. If a revival of ideology was contemplated, and if Communism was once again to make a major appeal to the non-
Communist left of emergent nations, it could not do it well if
the official histories of Marxism and socialism retained their
palpable absurdities. In a review of a book on the 1905 Moscow
soviet, the reviewer, sharing in the new wave of historical
honesty, felt constrained to point out that the author's pre-
1954 concept of party history led him to plain falsehoods, and
absurd ones at that.[4] Certainly it took some ingenuity on the
part of the author to discover that the Moscow soviet in 1905
was destroyed by the Trotskyites.[5] Leading roles in the creation of the soviets in that year were ascribed, among others, to
Stalin, Molotov, and Kuibyshev. The reviewer points out that
at the time Molotov was fifteen years old, and that Stalin and
Kuibyshev were, as anybody who read their biographies could
find out, away from the cities in which they were allegedly
leading the masses in the revolutionary struggle.[6] The Stalinist
school of history had not allowed for much in the way of mistake or change of opinion by the guiding saints of Communism,
and Kostomarov could write unblushingly that, from the very
beginning, the Soviet movement in 1905 had the support
and enthusiastic adherence of Lenin. Yet before 1955 Kostomarov's book would have been hailed as a valuable contribution; and in the condemnation of the new wave of historical
criticism in March 1957, it was the reviewer who was to be

condemned for his alleged denigration of the role of the Bolsheviks in 1905, and not the author, who had written absurdities and lies.

The scholarly discussion of the nature and development of socialist thought came to an effective end in the early thirties when Stalin in a celebrated dictum reprimanded the then leading party historian, Emelyan Yaroslavsky, for not realizing that the nonorthodox varieties of socialism represented not merely deviations but a betrayal of the working class. From then on, the non-Leninist offshoots of socialism (and of non-Stalinist ones in Bolshevik times) became simply a catalogue of epithets. The state of paralysis which gripped Soviet historical thought on the subject became reflected in a consequent weakening of the knowledge of the very principles of Marxism itself and, in fact, in the growth of ideological agnosticism and skepticism in the ranks of the party. The eventual danger to the regime was recognized even by Stalin when, in his *Economic Problems of Socialism in the USSR*, he deplored the lack of ideological preparation and Marxist education of incoming party recruits. The real answer of course could not be given by Stalin, because it would have required an end to Stalinism in history and ideology. His successors, for reasons indicated above, had to sanction and even push for a reopening of discussion of some problems which could not have been mentioned under the old tyrant. In this sense it was Khrushchev, Suslov, and Mikoyan who started what was later on branded by them as revisionism. The experiment was probably initiated with some realization of the danger inherent to the party and the regime, but the alternative was considered more dangerous.

In order to discuss the official ideology without wandering beyond the danger point, one must resort to circumlocutions. The Soviet historian in 1955 was called upon to show the richness and variety of Marxist traditions. But this "higher criticism" was not to intrude upon the essential infallibility of the doctrine of Marx and Engels, nor upon the uniqueness of its true modern interpretation, Leninism. An American writer who wants to criticize the prevailing system of the mixed economy without lapsing into the currently unfashionable plea for straightforward socialism will sometimes argue for an increase in public spending. Similarly, a Communist historian whose researches might lead him to question the standard view of the Leninist interpretation of Marxism in 1902 or 1917 may find his opening in the variety of views, positions, and hesitations current among the Marxists *before* the infallible dictum had been laid down.

In appraising the work of Soviet historians between the official encouragement of freer writing in 1955 and the damning of revisionism in March 1957, it is unnecessary to accept the official verdict that the "guilty" historians were engaged in a clandestine attack upon Leninism and Marxism or attempted to rehabilitate the Menshevik view of socialism. It makes much more sense to assume that they were trying loyally to squeeze as much as possible of historical truth into the framework of official dogma. It would be foolish to think that these people, some of them experienced academic bureaucrats, were motivated by any feeling of opposition to the regime or the ideology. And yet we must grant that there is an element of logic, even if a perverse one, in their subsequent condemnation. For in the historical sciences, just as in other spheres of Soviet life, the thaw threatened to have concrete and, from the point of view of the rulers, undesirable results.

Central to the legitimacy of Communist rule is the belief that the seizure of power in 1917 was in complete accordance with the Marxian canon. Indeed, the basis of the whole ideology rests upon two axioms: Marxism is the only true science of society, and the seizure of power by the Bolsheviks was the only correct application of Marxism in Russian conditions.

To question any element of Leninist tactics in 1917–18—rejection of parliamentarianism, suppression of the other revolutionary and socialist parties, confiscation of land and heavy industry—means not only to question the Marxist character of Leninism but also, by indirection, to criticize some of the basic political and economic features of the Soviet state. Furthermore, under Stalinism the official interpretation of Lenin's tactics insisted upon their absolute and unhesitating character: each major decision was not merely the result of a conjunction of events or pressures of one sort or another; it was in the given circumstance the proper and necessary application of Marxism. Those Bolsheviks who opposed Lenin at any crucial point were not exponents of different tactics or of a different brand of Marxism, but simply traitors and capitulators. The same was true of those foreign socialists who criticized as un-Marxist one or another aspect of the Bolshevik revolution.

It is in this light that one can understand the furor unleashed by a series of books and articles which, in the period under discussion, insisted that the historical reality of the years 1917–1918 was a bit more complicated than that presented in Stalin's *Short Course*. The most interesting among them, the most innocent in what it said and the one which aroused the most violent condemnation, was V. P. Nasirin's "Some Problems of the Socialist Transformation of Industry in the USSR." [7] The author simply restated what was well known by everybody who read the pre-1930 Soviet books on the subject: that the precipitous nationalization of heavy industry in the wake of the October Revolution was imposed upon the Bolshevik rulers, and that the previous Bolshevik program had envisaged a gradual and cautious plan of nationalization of the means of production. The author reclaimed the resolution of the Sixth Party Congress—again it could be found and read in Soviet libraries—which called for immediate nationalization of banks and syndicates but *not* of heavy industrial enterprises.[8] He recalled Lenin's misgivings about the workers' taking on the management of industrial enterprises and about the attrition of technical specialists. Carried away by his "discovery," the unfortunate seeker after historical truth quoted Marx's dictum on the ripening of socialism in the bosom of capitalism and Lenin's definition of socialism as "state capitalist monopoly turned to the benefit of the whole nation." [9]

Now there was nothing on the surface or in the substance of Nasirin's article to lead to the charge of heresy. The article did not challenge the October Revolution, nor did it detract from the picture of Lenin as a wise and far-seeing theorist and man of action. But in Soviet totalitarianism, even in its modified post-Stalin phase, we encounter the half-real, half-imaginary spheres of the hidden meaning and "where it all might lead to." And by the latter criteria this unsensational piece of historical research opened up frightening possibilities: the Bolshevik Party during the revolution evidently did not always act in perfect unison and harmony with the masses. On the contrary, a spontaneous movement of the workers imposed upon Lenin and his colleagues something they had shied away from: a premature nationalization of heavy industry. If so, to continue along this line, was the October Revolution a true Marxian revolution or a Blanquist coup d'état (a view held by "renegades" like Kautsky), with the Bolsheviks riding to power on a wave of anarchist disorders? To pursue Nasirin's line means not only to question the Marxist legitimacy of November but also to accept the doctrine of evolutionary socialism and the necessity of complete industrialization before socialism can take over. Hence, to shift to concrete political problems, why should there be Communist parties in underdeveloped or semi-industrialized countries? How can an ideological revival of

Communism in the USSR be strengthened by repeating the dictum that socialism is merely a state capitalist monopoly working for the benefit of the nation? It goes without saying that Nasirin's view was passed over after 1957. The new party history says in laconic fashion, "At the end of November 1917, the Soviet government turned to the nationalization of heavy capitalist industry." [10]

Nasirin's article was not the most celebrated deviation to emerge from the Pandora's box of freer historical criticism. More stir was created by Burdzhalov's articles on the Bolsheviks' tactics following the February Revolution. Actually Burdzhalov's views, on the whole more closely connected with actual party politics and of great interest to a historian of Bolshevism, are of less interest from the point of view of Soviet attitudes toward socialism.

In the blast to which the new historical outlook was subjected in March 1957, it was to be claimed that Burdzhalov's intent had been to denigrate Stalin and to bring back the names of Zinoviev and Kamenev into party history. It was clear from the articles that the historian's purpose was simply to remove some of the more glaring falsifications of the history of the party before October 1917 and that his criticism of Stalin nowhere approached the frightful revelations of Khrushchev's own speech. But by 1957 the Soviet leaders realized that revisionism had become one of the fruits of the iconoclastic campaign and that Stalin had to be restored to an honorable position, if not to his pre-1954 pedestal. Our interest in Burdzhalov's contribution lies in his indirect avowal of the relative flexibility and eclectic character of Bolshevism before April 1917. Again, the notion that there was only one "correct" line of Russian Marxism—it leaped out ready-made from Lenin's head in 1902, took on a concrete tactical form in 1914, and was adhered to by all true Bolsheviks (that is, except for the outright traitors like Zinoviev, Kamenev, and Rykov)—is confronted with the facts of history and found inexact. Unwittingly the author suggests that Bolshevism had not completely overcome its social-democratic heritage until Lenin's return in April 1917, that parliamentary and coalition impulses were not lacking among the Bolsheviks following February, and that perhaps the true Marxist tradition is broader and more inclusive than Leninism-Stalinism.

That the Marxist tradition is purely revolutionary and that it rejects parliamentarianism per se is, of course, the foundation stone of Leninism. It was, therefore, something of a challenge to point out that in March and April 1917 Lenin's own party was not quite sure whether Marxism did not require it to join with the other socialist parties, and to support temporarily the bourgeois-democratic Provisional Government. The slogan that the only legitimate organ of the people's will was to be found in the soviets, points out Burdzhalov, had come from the rank and file of the party. Their leadership vacillated on the subject of the Duma.[11] In many places the Bolsheviks were renewing their collaboration with the Mensheviks, and there was talk about the possibility of reunion of the two socialist parties. The author reminds his readers that, under the provisional leadership of Stalin and Kamenev, the Petrograd Bolsheviks turned still further toward the right and that the majority of the Petrograd Committee agreed with Kamenev when, on March 18, he characterized the talk about assuming power as premature.[12] The same note was sounded in the first reaction to Lenin's April theses: the bureau of the Central Committee rejected them and agreed with Kamenev's and Stalin's view that 1917 was not parallel to 1871 (the Paris Commune), but represented a revolutionary situation of the 1789 or 1848 form. Thus the skein of events in 1917 was infinitely more involved than that painted in the *Short Course*. It was not a simple and edifying tale of heroism, wisdom, and correct Marxism, on the one hand, and of betrayal and villainy, on the other; it was, among other things, a period during which some good Marxists had still not decided what was the proper Marxist solution for revolutionary Russia. The author leaves no doubt that it was Lenin who had the right formula, but before pointing that out he had said too much.

Viewed from one point of view, the period of thaw in historical criticism signified an effort to enlarge the legitimate sphere of Soviet historiography and to make the writing of history meaningful. Ever since the condemnation of the Pokrovsky school by Stalin, the limits of historical discussion, which after all is what distinguishes history from mere chronology, had been narrowed down almost to the point of disappearance. When it came to the history of political movements, the Soviet historian was reduced to the role of a copyist. Historical records and writings contradicting the official line (including even some of Stalin's writings before 1930) were locked away.[13] Under the spur of de-Stalinization the Soviet historian could begin (so it seemed between 1955 and 1957) to employ the tools of his trade and transcend mere recitation. It became possible to enlarge the scope of historical study. While Burdzhalov, Nasirin, and others pointed out the dissensions within the early Bolshevik ranks and thus suggested that even the Leninist version of Marxism was not, at first, monolithic but variegated, others could go back to the earlier periods of Marxism and again discover a multiplicity of tendencies and interpretations rather than a homogeneous science of revolution.

Even then, however, Soviet historiography could not take a cue from the tendency current among Western Marxists, one which found an echo in Poland, of stressing the voluntaristic and evolutionary element in Marxism at the expense of strict determinism and the revolutionary message. Instead, more emphasis was given to the connection of Marxism with other socialist and progressive groups and to those utterances of Marx indicating the possibility of a peaceful as distinguished from a violent and nonparliamentary revolution. Typical of this tendency is an article by B. A. Rozhov, "The Program of the Chartist Convention of 1851," mentioning Marx's statement of 1871 that England was one country where a socialist revolution could come about peacefully and legally.[14] The author concentrates on the relationship between Marxism and Chartism and stresses the master's conviction that the realization of the Charter in the England of the 1850s would have been equivalent to a revolution. Yet the Charter did not contain a single economic postulate, and the Chartist movement as a whole was very far from being socialist in any sense of the word. Here, then, is an attempt to anchor Marxism in the democratic and progressive tradition of the West, something, to be sure, in perfect accordance with the most orthodox view and yet suggestive of a new emphasis.[15]

Does the trend of 1955–1957 add up to revisionism in Soviet historiography? Two observations are relevant. In the first place, the noun itself, as is common with the frightful semantics of official Communism, obscures rather than clarifies what was going on. If by revisionism is meant a definite interpretation of Marxism associated with the name of Eduard Bernstein, a definite political philosophy and a view of history, then of course the timid attempts of historians had very little to do with it. They were writing in the spirit of what they blissfully conceived to be the new orthodoxy, eschewing and denouncing that other twin god of deviation, "sectarianism." If by revisionism is meant the phenomenon which occurs in the Marxist and Communist world whenever blinkers are removed and one is allowed to see that there are several Marxes and not just one, and that there are several roads to socialism and not just the one traversed by the Bolsheviks in 1917, then of course the

Soviet historians were participants in the revisionist movement led and abetted by Nikita Khrushchev and the Presidium of the Communist Party of the Soviet Union.

II

Soviet Communism finds itself in a profound ideological impasse. That impasse is masked, to be sure, by the great successes of the Soviet state and of the world Communist movement. The trouble can be best detected in the struggle the party has led against the half-phantom and half-reality of revisionism. The appearance of the latter, as observed above, was the consequence of the decision of the regime to disestablish the worst features of internal and external Stalinism. The decision represented a conviction that Communism was now a strong and vigorous ideology which no longer needed terror and excessive dogmatism as a protective shield, but could be counted upon to advance in the world because of its inherent superiority over Western liberalism. The "abolition" of the cult of personality was the first and decisive step in this *official* revisonism. Along with the cult, sectarianism and dogmatism were denounced. By admitting the legitimacy of Yugoslav Communism, by allowing a degree of autonomy to their satellites, the Soviet leaders sanctioned a multiplicity of roads to socialism and admitted that their own road was not necessarily the only one. But implicit in these concessions was the assumption that they would bring immediate and substantial gains to the regime. Yugoslavia would be drawn once again into the orbit of the Soviet Union. The satellites would now be bound to the USSR not only by force but also by gratitude and stronger ideological ties. And, most important, internally the reforms would be followed by a revitalization of ideology and a greater and more genuine rallying of all social forces around the party and the regime.

The external consequences of the denunciation of Stalinism

are well known. But less well understood are the repercussions of the new course inside the USSR. For all the regime's gains in popularity and efficiency, the ideological premises of Communism, as practiced in the Soviet Union, were put in question. The old dogmatism had at least concealed the contradictions between theory and practice. It did not allow the posing of the question, "What next?" and it did suggest that the mere questioning of the Marxist character of the Soviet state was an act of treason. It would be foolish to believe that the new discussions in history or the thaw in literature threatened the actual foundations of totalitarianism. But an uncurtailed debate about the sources of Marxism and Leninism, taken in conjunction with the concurrent events in Hungary and Poland, suggested that a new generation of intellectual "inner rebels" might arise in post-Stalin Russia. The regime acted speedily and firmly to check the undesirable tendencies. What prevented an earlier and sharper denunciation of revisionism was probably the continuing split in the highest party councils which lasted through the summer of 1957. Even before the question of leadership was definitely settled, the party early in 1957 took steps to curtail historical criticism of the accepted (up to 1955) views of ideology and party history. By resolution of the Central Committee, the editorial board of the official historical journal was purged and submitted to closer party control; the scope of discussion was narrowed down and the historian deprived of most of the gains of the preceding few years. As a matter of fact, the change of the course required a redefinition of the historian's task which, in its openness and its clear directive to subjugate history writing to the needs of propaganda, went beyond the most Stalinist strictures. History for history's sake was definitely condemned. Insofar as socialism was concerned, the assigned task of Soviet historiography became to expose revisionism, to show the organic connection between every departure from the line advocated by the Russian party and the theories and views advocated sixty years before by Bernstein and his followers. This task, to revert to Soviet semantics, has been honorably discharged by the Soviet historians. A veritable flood of books and articles has made of revisionism an *omnium gatherum* of every type of criticism of the Soviet Union, any theory of nonrevolutionary Marxism and any plea against the monopoly of power by a socialist party. In the ranks of revisionism have been found persons as diverse as Harold Laski, John Gates, Leon Blum, and Marshal Tito. It yet remains for an ingenious Soviet historian to close the circle of deviationism by asserting that sectarianism itself is in essence a species of revisionism, and to discover that Malenkov, Molotov, and Kaganovich were really revisionists masquerading as Stalinists.

It would be a mistake to think that the new trend is a reversion, pure and simple, to the pre-1953 days. One concrete gain has been preserved, and that is the possibility of describing, to be sure from a specific and prefabricated point of view, views and materials which in Stalin's days were simply not fit subjects for discussion. In being called upon to condemn various perversions of Marxism, the historian still has the opportunity to display the richness and variety of the socialist tradition. His treatment, though biased, can no longer stop at mere vilification or contain obvious absurdities. It is unlikely that a new treatment of the revolutionary movement of 1905 would find there the Trotskyites and their wrecking activities. History, like other branches of intellectual activity in Khrushchev's Russia, is expected to conform, but at a more intelligent level than under Stalin.

The difficulty in meeting the new requirements is well illustrated in a "review" by E. P. Kandel of some recent Western literature on Marxism.[16] The title—"The Perversion of Marx's and Engels' Struggle for a Proletarian Party in the Works of Some Right Socialists"—suggests the style of polemic, taking one's mind back to such classics of the Reformation as *The First Blast of the Trumpet Against the Monstrous Regiment of Women*, but the style and the cogency of argument are, unfortunately, inferior to John Knox's. Kandel has taken a rather motley assembly of authors (including Boris Nikolaevsky, Maximilien Rubel, and Harold Laski) to task for suggesting an evolutionary view of Marx's philosophy after 1849. The article is typical in its melange of *ad hominem* arguments and what is known as scholarly discussion. The main theme is the thesis going back as far as Bernstein that, after the *Communist Manifesto*, Marx began to eschew purely revolutionary tactics. This view, which contrasts the brief revolutionary period of 1847–1849 with Marx's mainly humanitarian theories earlier and evolutionary ones afterwards, has become something of a fad among Western socialists. It has also been heard behind the Iron Curtain in the writings of Leszek Kolakowski and other Polish Communists. Needless to say, it has become one of the main targets of the campaign against revisionism.

It is indisputable that the weakest part of the attempt to democratize Marx is to call as witness his writings and notes of the years before 1847, when he was still groping for a philosophy of history. But our author cannot forgo the argument that Nikolaevsky's views are false simply because of his anti-Communist activities.[17] Nor can he refrain from protesting too much, as in his assertion that the Communist historian exhibits exemplary scholarship precisely because of his devotion to the party. What is striking is that, rather than dismissing the argument of "humanitarian Marxism" because it rests on evidence predating the formation of Marxism as a cohesive system, the writer feels constrained to deny clear evidence. Marx could not be as much against Blanqui as Nikolaevsky claims, since Blanqui in 1848 defended the interests of the French proletariat. And Rubel would make Marx into a kind of Leon Blum. As much as one sympathizes with the Soviet author's point of view, one cannot describe his arguments as scholarly or convincing. Here and there he strikes a more reasonable note. And, to be sure, of what weight are the early scribblings of Marx in appraising his whole system as compared with the Anti-Duhring? But these are small islands of genuine scholarly polemic in a sea of invective, and Rubel is finally dismissed as a plagiarist.[18]

If such a relatively weak interpretation of Marxism, in its own way as onesided as the Leninist one, is combated so clumsily and on a personal level, then what counterargument will meet a more serious assault upon orthodoxy? One can dig very deeply into Marx's writings and still not find a plea for one-party dictatorship. On the other hand, Marx's approval of the Paris Commune would imply that even the dictatorship of the proletariat did not preclude a many-party system. This delicate point is excised from Harold Laski's 1948 introduction to the *Communist Manifesto*.[19] Why Laski is taken as an exponent of contemporary revisionism, and why a more typical work of his is not selected for discussion, can be a mystery only to those who do not understand that, in a review of this kind, a sort of national symmetry has to be preserved and that the main Western powers have to be represented. Thus Laski is arraigned alongside the representative of French revisionism, Rubel, and the German and American sufferers from the same disease, Landshut and Nikolaevsky. Laski's argument is disposed of by a rhetorical question: Why does the Labour Party refuse to let the British Communists become affiliated with it?

Why is there this idiotic compulsion to register the most diverse forms of activity—political, literary, and philosophical —and the most diverse types of personalities—a former Menshevik, a Labourite, and people who have never been Marxists and consequently have nothing to "revise"—under the common rubric of revisionism? It is difficult to answer this, except by the supposition that whenever history becomes a part of propaganda its task opposes that of scholarly history: it has to oversimplify, obscure vital differences, and paint in the garish colors of socialist realism. During the period of relaxation, many Soviet historians began to say that certain elements of the doctrine and history of the socialist movement were somewhat more complicated than had hitherto been believed. Now a historian, Chagin in 1959, begins his account of real revisionism as follows: "The analysis of revisionism which arose in the nineties of the nineteenth century shows vividly its identity, both in theory and in practice, with the views of contemporary revisionism. The latter represents, in essence, the newest type of Bernsteinism, revived and adjusted according to the new historical conditions." [20] It is a formula as clear-cut and suitable for the catechism of a party instructor as the answer to the question, "What is Leninism?"—"Leninism is the Marxism of the era of imperialism."

Another reason for using Bernstein to dispose of Marshal Tito, Western socialists, and the Polish would-be reformers of Marxism lies in the doctrinal and scholastic character of the official Soviet creed. Bernstein's views were condemned by Lenin and rejected officially by the German Social Democratic Party. Hence all new revisionism was in advance rejected by the father of Communism and has no scriptural authority. The burden of discussion is very seldom placed on the nature of the old or new deviation, but consists of a string of citations from the authorities: Marx, Engels, and Lenin. A sample of the argument will render its flavor:

Already then [in 1893] Bernstein and Kautsky conceded to international opportunism. For instance, they removed from a work of Eleanor Aveling, *The Elections in Great Britain,* the correct characterization of the Fabians as opportunists. Engels most resolutely protested against that, pointing to the sympathies of Bernstein for the English opportunists. He opposed Kautsky's attempt to entrust to Bernstein the writing of an article about the socialist movement in England. Engels did not believe Bernstein and his revolutionary common sense did not deceive him.[21]

It is clear that the author projects the atmosphere and phraseology of Soviet Communism into the life of the international socialist movement of the 1890s. It is 1893, but the "opportunists" and "capitulators" at large are being tracked down by socialist vigilance, by people like Engels, Lenin, and Plekhanov. There is no attempt to present *in extenso* the arguments of Bernstein and those of his followers or to discuss their substance. The technique employed is to list the bare outlines of revisionism, to note the sympathetic reactions to it of liberal and bourgeois circles in Germany, and to spear it with a quotation from Rosa Luxemburg, Liebknecht, or Lenin. It is hard in a sense to classify Chagin's treatment of revisionism as history; it is, rather, a projection of Soviet politics into the German social-democratic scene at the turn of the century. Since Kautsky was to attack the October Revolution, the author, for instance, cannot let it out that in the period under discussion Kautsky was for Lenin the leading interpreter of Marxism. Even the strongest opponents of revisionism, such as Rosa Luxemburg, are criticized for their toleration of Bernstein and the failure to eject him from the party.[22] That, for all their revolutionary interpretation of Marxism and militancy, Rosa Luxemburg, Liebknecht, and others like them simply did not possess the mentality suitable for purges, recantations, and *ex cathedra* pronouncements is a matter of regret and a reflection on their inferior brand of Marxism.

In its rigidity and perversions of historical truth, the attack upon revisionism also reflects another aspect of contemporary Soviet politics. Original revisionism was not a diabolical invention of Bernstein or Vollmar, but a response to the facts of political and economic life which made many of the theorems and conclusions of Marx based on the study of capitalist England of the 1840s and 1850s inapplicable to Germany of the end of the century. And in a sense, the Russia of the fifties and sixties of this century has faced a similar development. The message of Marxism-Leninism had been found convincing in the 1917 Revolution. The logic of Marxism had provided the impetus behind the drive toward industrialization and modernization which occupied most of the Stalin era. But what is the message of Marxism now? The very incoherence with which the Communist leaders try to spell out the meaning of the transition to Communism which the USSR is allegedly undertaking at present is a testimony of how little relevance to the actual conditions of an industrialized society is contained in the old doctrine.

In this very broad sense revisionism, if we want to call it that, is a recurrent phenomenon, and not only in Marxism. It recurs whenever ruling doctrines no longer offer clear goals for the future; the ideology then has to be liberalized and alternatives to it allowed or it has to be frozen into a dogma preserved by repression and indoctrination. The German Social Democrats in condemning their revisionism made impossible any collaboration with the liberal elements which might have transformed Imperial Germany into a parliamentary democracy, while, at the same time, the nonrevolutionary temper of the German worker refused to let him follow the radical program of the party. The Soviet leaders arrested the process of liberalization when they judged that it was starting to threaten the Communist dogma and, in the long run, their totalitarian system. But by doing so they have not restored or imparted new vigor and meaning to their doctrine. It would be hard to see the initiation of the comrades' courts and the abolition of the state committee on sports as the first tokens of the "withering away" of the state and the first symptoms of Communist society. The recent steps against some marginal elements of private property still prevalent in the Soviet Union are but a feeble swing of the pendulum in the never-ending alternation between the policies of incentives and of egalitarianism, a decisive turn toward the latter being quite unthinkable in a modern industrial state.

But if, internally, Marxism-Leninism has little to offer, in the world at large it is still an ideology and a technique of revolution and industrialization with tremendous powers of attraction. To that extent, the foreign successes of Soviet Communism have obscured, on the domestic scene, the relative uselessness of the doctrine and its sole remaining function as a rationale for totalitarianism. The struggle against revisionism is, then, a struggle on a world scale, and one of its most important aspects is the fight against "excessive" claims for autonomy by other Communist parties. Needless to say, this is one aspect of modern revisionism which has very little to do with original revisionism. Eduard Bernstein, an advocate of democratic socialism and of internationalism, would consider it an insult to be branded as the patron saint of essentially totalitarian and nationalistic Yugoslav Communism. Revisionism has also become a euphemism for any tendency on the part of a Communist party to claim a degree of *ideological* as well as political independence from Moscow. It has come to denote any socialism or radicalism which opposes Communism.

The ideological consolidation within the Communist bloc was necessitated by the loosening of the purely administrative and police methods of controlling the Soviet empire that occurred after Stalin's death. An additional factor of great importance has been the emergence of new states, most of them unindustrialized and therefore ideal areas for the spread of radical philosophies and movements. It became important that no other brand of radicalism but the one stamped "approved by Moscow" be allowed to claim the heritage of Marxism. When the attempts to reintegrate Yugoslavia into the Communist camp bore indirect results in the form of the Polish disorders and the Hungarian revolt, Titoism again had to be cast out. The program of the Communist League of Yugoslavia, which the Soviets condemned as revisionist in 1958, contained nothing that was not implicit in Titoism in 1955 and 1956, when the Soviet regime hailed it so enthusiastically as a legitimate form of Communism.

The Soviet historian's task became correspondingly to reappraise those elements of the history of radical thought which could suggest a variety of permissible approaches to socialism or hint at a greater latitude in Marxism than that currently allowed by Soviet Communism. There has been, for instance, a general downgrading of any and all socialist thinkers in the West who cannot be associated with an unqualified approval of the October Revolution and of the Soviet state. Kautsky appears now not merely as a renegade from socialism following his reaction to the revolution, but as a man who from the very earliest days of his activity inclined toward revisionism.[23] Those reading a 1957 work on German socialism during the First World War will discover with only the greatest difficulty that Bernstein and Kautsky occupied during the war an anti-militarist position.[24] Even the Spartakists are severely reprimanded for their democratic scruples, for their neglect to organize (before November 1917!) a purely revolutionary party apart from the Independent Socialists, as well as for their occasional pacifist scruples.[25] In other words, even the most radical socialist movement is judged by the yardstick of the behavior of the Bolshevik Party, or rather by what the official party histories after the 1930s represented as the behavior and ideology of the Bolsheviks in 1917. The Spartakists are even reproached for their lack of faith after February, when they believed that a socialist revolution in Russia could survive only if supported by successful workers' revolutions elsewhere.

The same claim for the uniqueness of the Bolshevik formula

is inherent in the Soviet historian's approach to the non-Marxist socialist movements. The traditional Marxian view has held "nonscientific" socialism to be a preliminary if misconceived step in the achievement of class consciousness by the proletariat, a product of the very conditions which later would bring about Marxism. It was in this spirit that Marx and Engels hailed the left wing of Chartism, or for that matter various radical and even nationalist movements on the Continent. For all of its polemical tone, classical Marxism believed in historicism, that the stages of economic development are reflected in corresponding periods of social thought. The decision ending Stalinism in historical research called for, among other things, a wider teaching and research on the precursors of Marxism and Leninism, for an end of the obscurantism which would apply to historiography the formula of politics, "Who is not with us is against us." But the more recent period has brought back the tendency to lump together all forms of non-Marxian socialism as being in effect anti-Marxian and directed against the Soviet Union (sometimes even before the latter existed). In dealing with Fabian socialism, the Soviet writer proclaims that the Fabian Society right from its creation led the struggle against Marxism.[26] He is unembarrassed by the fact that Marxism was almost nonexistent in England at the time of the appearance of the first Fabian essays and that most of their authors had not in all likelihood read a single line of Marx. The author in discussing *contemporary* English socialism keeps reverting to G. D. H. Cole's youthful Guild Socialism as if, in 1959, it were still a vital part of the philosophy of the Labour Party.

The sum total of the Soviet appraisal of modern socialism is, then, vitiated by the tendency to find the enemy, revisionism, in the most unlikely places and in the most unrelated theories and phenomena. As often happens in such cases, the nature and the causes of what might with some justification be called genuine modern revisionism became obscured.

The main expressions of this revisionism were not to be found in Yugoslavia, where alleged revisionism is really a euphemism for Tito's unwillingness to subordinate his foreign policy to that of the Soviet Union, but rather among some Polish and Italian Communists and left-wing socialists. It was there that the shock of the disclosures about Stalinism led to a theoretical reappraisal of Leninism and even of Marxism. In Poland this reappraisal never went beyond vague talk about the humanitarian rather than deterministic essence of Marxism. In Italy, however, a greater variety of theoretical divergences infiltrated into the discussions, and it is Italy—where, for a time, the highest party functionaries hesitated before the new views—that is of the greatest interest to the student of modern revisionism.

The essence of Bernstein's views consisted in his assault on the doctrine of the gradual worsening of the lot of the working class under capitalism and on the general Marxian notion that the exploiting essence of capitalism is unchangeable. It is this common-sense critique of Marx's proposition that Bernstein made the cornerstone of his system, and it enabled him to develop further arguments with the classical Marxian views of the state, the class war, and so on. This is the element which marks genuine revisionism and distinguishes it from criticisms of the Soviet Union's foreign policy or of the details of organization of the Communist state, all of which have been pushed by Soviet writers into the same pit.

In dealing with the aberrant Italian Communists, a 1959 Soviet publication obscures the theoretical element of their protest and reduces it to a breach of party discipline and opposition to the Soviet Union's leading role in the socialist camp. The source of Italian revisionism, the author helpfully explains, lies in the "maximalist" tradition of Italian Marxism (that is, the very opposite of democratic socialism). Superficially maximalism indicates an uncompromising revolutionary posture, but in fact it leads to the loosening of party discipline and to waiting for a spontaneous revolution by the masses. From there the road leads very clearly to deviations like those of a former Communist, now a Nenni Socialist, A. Giolitti. The latter has defied the true Marxist position that the state is but an instrument of monopoly capitalism, holding that the bourgeois state may challenge the monopolies.[27] He has disputed the "immiserization" canon and in general has fallen under the guidance of bourgeois critics of Marxism.[28] The author's criticism of the Nenni Socialists is extensive but subdued. For all the luxuriant growth of heresies among them, they remain allied with the Communists. But the range of their deviations is truly amazing: from Nenni's stress on individual freedom to Lelio Basso's proposal to renounce Leninism as the basis of revolutionary socialism.[29]

What is characteristic of the discussion of modern socialism is the attrition of its intellectual content. After all, original revisionism found worthy opponents and scholarly counter-arguments in Rosa Luxemburg, Kautsky, and Hilferding. Their contemporary successor, if he does not simply resort to epithets, dismisses the revisionist or pseudo-revisionist argument as a token of hostility to the Soviet Union or by a simple fiat from Lenin or (much less frequently) Marx or Engels. The hunt for unorthodoxy, though not as brutal and primitive as in Stalin's time, is equally all-inclusive. Such a scholar of undoubted Marxist orthodoxy and high standing as Jurgen Kuczynski is assailed for stating a simple historical fact that the "masses" in Germany at the beginning of World War I were pervaded by patriotic rather than revolutionary sentiments and that the Social Democrats in voting for the war credits were responding to popular pressure.[30] What there is of a genuine intellectual argument is appalling in its primitiveness. In combating John Strachey's and Benedict Kautsky's old refrain about immiserization, the author flatly denies that Marx and Engels postulated an *absolute* decline of the worker's standard of living,[31] but he is incapable of putting forth a coherent alternative interpretation.

III

A student of Soviet historiography is unavoidably recalled to the same question which faces the analyst of any sphere of Soviet life: how much of a basic change has there been in the last decade, and has it been real or illusory? In historiography, as in other areas, it is much too simple to see the developments as following one cycle: repression, liberalization after Stalin's death, and then a retrogression beginning in 1957, carrying the situation back to where it was in 1953. The Soviet historian now is certainly no freer than he was under Stalin to arrive at any conclusions to which his researches might lead him. If a student of Russia's beginnings still feels constrained to see in the "Norman" theory an invention of Western reactionaries designed to suggest that the Slavs are incapable of ruling themselves, then it is unreasonable to expect an objective study of Bernstein, the Russian populists, or Guild Socialism.

Nevertheless, there has been a change. If Stalin's period was the Dark Age of Soviet historiography, as of intellectual life in general, then the present might be compared to the Counter Reformation. The historian is not only supposed to restate and repeat; he now engages in active polemic, both with his confreres in the West and, insofar as our subject is concerned, with the non-Communist socialists of the past.

What pervades Soviet historical science is an awareness of both the greater opportunities and the greater ideological dangers facing Soviet Communism. For the first time since the millenarian days after the October Revolution, revolutionary Marxism appears ready to triumph on a world scale. At the same time, the future meaning of Communism in the Soviet Union and its relation to the views and policies of the Chinese Communists foreshadows basic and on the surface insoluble problems. These dilemmas are reflected not only in the official speeches and joint declarations of the Communist parties, but also in the day-to-day work of the Soviet historian and philosopher. Superficially it might appear that Bernstein might be safely relegated to the curiosa of intellectual history and that a catalogue of Rosa Luxemburg's merits need not always be accompanied by a mention of her basic "errors." But, although neither revisionism nor Luxemburgism threatens to sweep the Soviet Union, they pose questions and raise problems concerning the role of the Soviet Union in the international Communist movement and the role of the totalitarian party in a socialist society. The struggle against revisionism is not so much a struggle against an actual ideology as it is a prophylactic campaign designed to prevent the erection of ideological shelters for present and future political discontent.

How far is the present state of Soviet historiography the product of genuine indoctrination, and how far is it a consequence of opportunism (in our bourgeois-democratic sense of the word)? The testimony of 1955–1957 is fairly instructive on this count. When for a while it appeared safe to write a more professional type of history, even on subjects as perilous as that of the history of the Communist Party and of international socialism, there was no shortage of historians who both in their conclusions and in their use of materials demonstrated their willingness to be historians in a more genuine sense of the term. To be sure, they were writing not in protest but to fulfill what they assumed to be a new directive. Their example, however, shows how imperfectly even the most efficient dictatorship can stamp out the drive for historical truth.

7 KHRUSHCHEV AND BOCCACCIO

It is on the first day in *The Decameron* that the story is told of Abraham the Jew who, importuned by his friend to become a Christian and hesitant to do so, goes to Rome to study Christianity. His Christian friend is ready to concede the game: no one can observe the real state of affairs in the center of the Christian world and yet arrive at the conviction of the divine mission of the Church. Abraham returns appalled at the corruption and degeneracy he had found, but his conclusion is the very opposite of his friend's fears: an institution whose highest representatives are so corrupt and weak and which yet "continually increaseth and waxeth still brighter and more glorious" [1] must be divinely ordained. And Abraham becomes a Christian.

It is unlikely that members of the Presidium of the Central Committee of the Communist Party of the Soviet Union read Boccaccio for amusement or instruction. But the intended effect of the Twenty-Second Congress of the Communist Party in October–November 1961 does not fall short of Boccaccio's paradox: between 1934 and 1953 Soviet Russia grew enormously in power and influence. Communism, from its confinement in a single and backward country, grew to become the ruling creed of one third of mankind. Yet during the same period Russia and world Communism were guided, so his present-day successors allege, by a criminal psychopath, who without compunction dispatched his closest associates to death, tolerated and abetted a wholesale terror in all ranks of society, and exacted an adulation and worship for the likes of which one has to reach back to the reign of the most malevolent of the Roman emperors. The lesson, though its details are deeply disturbing, must yet be of comfort to a true believer. The forces of history must be behind Communism, for what other system could have survived and emerged stronger from so much criminality and suffering?

To a more skeptical mind, the Twenty-Second Congress presents problems of a different and rather prosaic nature. What reasons motivated the rulers of Russia in presenting their subjects with these horrible revelations, and what does the tale itself and the manner of its presentation mean to us in appraising the recent past and the future prospects of Communism? The two problems are closely connected.

I

The "revelations" at the Twenty-Second Congress can be grouped under three headings. First, there were further details about the crimes and atrocities of Stalin, which were not provided in Khrushchev's secret speech at the Twentieth Congress in 1956. Substantively, these do not add much to the picture painted in 1956, though this time Khrushchev clearly alleges that Stalin was implicated in Kirov's murder in 1934. But in tone of attack, there is a world of difference between the two recitals. The 1956 speech, never publicly released, described Stalin as a great statesman who, although becoming increasingly psychopathic and irresponsible after 1934, had only strayed from his early greatness. The 1961 indictments, despite some attempt to distinguish between the pre- and post-1934 Stalin, add up to the picture of a man cunning and unprincipled from the beginning of his career. Khrushchev emphasized Lenin's letter in 1922 which demanded Stalin's replacement as Secretary General.[2] There is thus, this time, a clear inconsistency in maintaining that Stalin had still rendered "great services" and in allowing his remains to rest, if not in the Mausoleum, then in a place of honor at the Kremlin wall.

The second element of the story consists in the exposure, and this is quite new, of the evil role played during the purges and atrocities of the thirties and forties by Stalin's close collaborators, especially by Malenkov, Molotov, Kaganovich, and, to a lesser extent, Voroshilov. At the Twentieth Congress, Stalin's leading subordinates, with the obvious exception of Beria, had been presented as victims rather than willing accomplices, and the revelations were made in the name of the whole leadership, which included the very people who in 1961 were exposed as criminals. Two details are quite piquant in this connection: Khrushchev had shed tears in relating the indignities heaped in Stalin's last years upon the aged Marshal Voroshilov, branded five years later along with the rest. And, as revealed in Khrushchev's concluding remarks on October 30, 1961, the chairman of the commission appointed in 1956 to investigate still further the crimes of the Stalin era was none other than Molotov.

Now, Molotov especially, but Malenkov, Kaganovich, and Voroshilov (he least of all) as well, were pictured as having had criminal personalities of their own. They all helped and abetted Stalin in his crimes. Malenkov was presented as the main executor of the Leningrad purges in 1949. Kaganovich was said to have performed similar tasks in the Ukraine, where after the war he replaced for a brief time Khrushchev as First

Secretary. (In what might well have been an anti-Semitic allusion, the present head of the Ukraine, Podgorny, referred sarcastically to Kaganovich's having posed as the "leader of the Ukrainian nation.") Voroshilov helped Stalin to massacre the ranks of the generals in 1937-38. And Molotov is singled out as the most pernicious man in the pre-1953 Soviet Union next to the "genial leader of mankind" himself. Those of Stalin's lieutenants who had disappeared some time ago are passed over lightly, except for casual bits of information like Beria's killing of a secretary of the Armenian Communist Party with his own hands. But in general not much is added to our knowledge of the roles played by Zhdanov, Beria, or Yezhov, and not a word is said about Poskrebyshev, the head of Stalin's personal secretariat during the tyrant's last years. The main fire is concentrated on the survivors of Stalin's closest entourage, with the understandable exceptions of Khrushchev and Mikoyan.

One is struck by the emphasis on the wanton criminality of both Stalin and his four aides. Molotov has a minor car accident while on a trip in Siberia—immediately some innocent people's heads roll. Stalin becomes envious of the popularity of Voznesensky's book about the wartime economy of the USSR, and the unfortunate author loses not only his party and state positions but his life.* We see the effort to prove not only that the accused were people who committed political mistakes and crimes, but that they were and are disgusting bestial characters. Who can listen without horror to the story of Yakir, one of the eight Soviet generals condemned in 1937 by a secret

* Ilyichev's speech, reported in *Pravda*, October 26, 1961. One is willing, indeed, to believe the worst about the people under discussion, but Ilyichev's accusation goes a bit too far. No one who has read Voznesensky's dull and ponderous book, with its adulatory references to Stalin in practically every paragraph, would see in it a fit object of an author's envy. As with Khrushchev's statement in 1956 that Stalin planned wartime campaigns on a globe, so with Ilyichev one feels that a good case is spoiled by exaggeration.

court martial? In his letter to the Presidium, the condemned commander, a hero of the civil war and once a favorite of Stalin's, wrote that were he to die it would be still with words of love for Stalin and the party. This petition was annotated by Stalin, recounts Shelepin, the head of the secret police, with the words "scoundrel and prostitute," and by Kaganovich with words that, the youthful successor to Yezhov and Beria assures the congress, could not be repeated in a public place.[3] Many similar details are adduced. The revelations about Stalin's crimes and those of his closest collaborators render feeble and ineffective even the most arduous Western attempts to depict the horrors of Stalinism. For it is clear that we see here not cruelty and inhumanity at the service of a great social or political mission, no Dostoyevskian Grand Inquisitor sacrificing the happiness of human beings for his dream of the historical purpose of mankind, but simply violent and nasty criminality, the products of sadism, envy, and fear, and the results of unbridled power. The imaginative efforts of Koestler and Serge, and the reach for some rationale, even a perverse one, of terror by a Deutscher or a Maynard, stand revealed as wide of the mark. The truth is simpler and more vulgar.

Nor can the motives for Khrushchev's and his group's denunciation of Stalin be found solely in reasons of state or in the political and ideological machinations which had taken place since the old despot died. There is, at least in Khrushchev's own pronouncements on the subject, a note of both horror and fascination: the awe at Stalin's feats of social engineering such as the collectivization drive of 1929–1933, which is still credited as a positive achievement even though it claimed more human sacrifices than the terror of the middle and late thirties; the secret satisfaction in Stalin's smooth destruction of all opposition and the establishment of the very pattern of totalitarianism of which the present First Secretary is a beneficiary, since it enables him by its very firmness and completeness to play the role of a "liberal" by pruning the Stalinist model of its pathological and terroristic excesses. It thus becomes psychologically understandable how, for the present-day rulers, the 1956 version of Stalin as a "bad man but a good thing" became insufficient. As with Boccaccio's convert, the very criminality of the heads of the cult reinforces the argument of the dogma. In his concluding speech to the party congress, Khrushchev dwelt again on Stalin's sadism and, as if the previous examples had not been enough, charged his predecessor with the murder of his brother-in-law and implied very strongly his complicity in the assassination of Kirov. And then came an incident at once macabre and childish in its conception: the ejection of Stalin's remains from the Mausoleum.

The third group of disclosures at the 1961 congress touches on the intraparty struggles since Stalin's death and concerns the "antiparty" group of Molotov, Malenkov, and Kaganovich, enlarged at times by Voroshilov, Shepilov, and a few others. This group of revelations and accusations must be approached with utmost caution. We are dealing with an attempt, certainly not new in Soviet history, to attribute a wide variety of political sins and crimes to a defeated faction which is not allowed to state its own case. We have in addition, it is fair to say, a deliberate attempt on the part of the victorious group to present all elements of opposition to it as a part of a definite criminal plot, and to charge the accused with additional crimes of commission or intent which, whether true or not, are bound to make a telling impression on the public mind. Thus, though it is quite clear that Molotov, Malenkov, and Kaganovich had long opposed Khrushchev and attempted with the help of others to unseat him in 1957, it is much less clear that they also were, as charged, uncompromising enemies of de-Stalinization or that Molotov had become the spokesman of the Albanian and Chinese viewpoint on international affairs. It is even less probable that those who joined the Evil Three in the abortive attempt to fire Khrushchev in June 1957—Saburov, Bulganin, Pervukhin, and others—shared their alleged heresies. It was on the face of it a simple maneuver to get rid of the First Secretary, and it was attempted by various people with various motives, some undoubtedly ideological, others personal in character.

This technique of guilt by association and extension in time and place presents several interesting points of comparison with its original model exhibited in the purge trials of the thirties. There a heterogeneous assembly of people, politicians, doctors, policemen, was charged and made to confess to the most varied and, much of the time, improbable collection of villainies and crimes. The huge canvas of treason was painted with a surrealistic profusion of detail: Bukharin plotting against Lenin's life in 1918, Yagoda making sure of his advancement by arranging that his predecessor should inhale sulphurous fumes while at work, "enemies of the people" mixing nails with butter to discredit collectivization. Nothing was spared in vilifying the accused as well as in establishing useful propaganda lessons. The sufferings and privations of the collectivization period were represented not as a consequence of the regime's brutality, but as the results of the diabolical activities of the Trotskyites and Bukharinites. We are in the presence of the Plot—an immemorial device of dogma-ridden political systems and groups which cannot conceive of political dissent, accident, or human inefficiency except as manifestations of planned and coordinated treason and malevolence.

To be sure, the accusations against the antiparty group have been free of the fantastic and clearly pathological elements of the purge trials. Nor have we yet encountered the ghastly mechanism of confessions and judicial assassinations. This, of course, is a reflection of the difference between Stalin's and Khrushchev's Russia. But there has been a very similar tendency to load the defeated party faction with every imaginable political sin and to make the charges not with regard to the truth but to the propaganda needs of the regime. For an outside observer, it becomes extremely difficult to separate the facts from fiction or exaggeration.

The hard core of undeniable fact centers on the meeting of the Presidium in June 1957 when Khrushchev, fresh from a visit to Finland, was dismissed from his post of First Secretary. The Twenty-Second Congress gave the first full confirmation of the fact that the vote on the question was seven to four among the full members of the Presidium, with only Suslov, Mikoyan, and Kirichenko standing with Khrushchev. The ancient symbol of the Communist style of sarcasm, parentheses, accompanies references to this "arithmetical majority," but, parentheses or no, the fact is that Khrushchev was dismissed by a majority of his colleagues and that the method of his dismissal, while not in accordance with the statutes of the party, followed a practice of long standing. (It is extremely doubtful whether the *initial* decisions to remove Beria or Zhukov were undertaken by the full complement of the Central Committee.)

The next act of the June 1957 drama has some members of the Central Committee, aroused by the rumors, literally beating on the doors of the Kremlin where the Presidium session was taking place. Bulganin's personal bodyguards attempted to bar their access but, after a heated discussion within the Presidium, a session of the full Central Committee was agreed upon. There of course the verdict was reversed and the would-be purgers purged themselves.

The minutes of the Central Committee meeting of June 1957 have not been released. The manner of telling the story of these crucial days has followed another weird Soviet custom: it is told in installments, each successive official version revealing an additional plotter or plotters—Bulganin's role in the intrigue was not broadcast until December 1958, Saburov's and Pervu-khin's in January 1959. And Voroshilov was allowed to stay as President of the USSR, for three years after the June crisis. It was only at the Twenty-Second Congress that the old veteran was abused and vilified, and Khrushchev combined a plea for leniency for the old man with a barbed reminder of how Voroshilov, now downcast and apologetic, fell to the intrigue with zest during the June days as if he were leading a cavalry charge.[4]

What united seven people so diverse in background in their determination to remove Khrushchev? The official answer is that they and Shepilov, who though only an alternate member of the Presidium was also somehow involved in the plot, opposed the de-Stalinization policies. Here it is much more difficult to follow the official version. It is credible up to a point that Molotov and Kaganovich felt the attacks upon Stalin also to be directed against them. Khrushchev rather disingenuously told the anecdote of how, when the crimes of the Stalin era were being brought to light and Molotov and Kaganovich would express horror, he would ask them why they had not protested when Stalin was alive. (It is not difficult to imagine what their answer must have been.) But everything points to the fact that a course of de-Stalinization represented the consensus of the whole leadership on the morrow of the despot's death. When Malenkov was removed as Chairman of the Council of Ministers in 1955, the gravamen of the charges preferred against him was that he favored the consumer industries, that is, he tried to carry out too much de-Stalinization in the economic field. Mention has already been made of how Voroshilov had been subjected to chicanery and persecution in Stalin's last years.

Nor is the legend of the Stalinism of the defeated faction confirmed by all of the official spokesmen. Kuusinen gave probably the most plausible explanation when he stated that what united the opposition was simply the desire to seize power.[5] Some of the plotters must have had perfectly clear and understandable reasons for disliking the First Secretary. His economic reforms announced in February 1957 had undercut the positions of Pervukhin and Saburov. Others must have been distressed by his tacit suppression of the principle of collective leadership, his constant improvisations in economic and foreign policies which led to the costly experiment of settling the virgin lands and contributed to the near disasters of Poland and Hungary in the fall of 1956. In other words, the opposition came together because of a combination of grievances and postulates which in no way can be summarized as Stalinism. The latter term or its euphemistic substitute, the cult of personality, has, like Trotskyism in the past, become a catchall for political abuse.

Why was the whole unsavory business of 1957 brought to light and rehashed? What credit could the party derive from revealing to the world once again its sordid past? From the mouths of their highest leaders the Soviet people heard how the most important problems of politics were solved in a manner reminiscent of Chicago gangland, how a former foreign minister and party secretary, Shepilov, employed personal blackmail to secure his political ends. Quite apart from the crimes of Stalinism, the post-Stalin era of Soviet politics has scarcely been presented in a favorable light. We cannot explain the revelations by assuming that the erstwhile opposition still represents a political danger to the current leadership. Nor is it reasonable to read international implications into an essentially domestic problem. To be sure, Kuusinen hinted that Molotov tried to fish in the muddy waters not only at home but also abroad, and foreign commentators took the remark as they were expected, to mean that he was seeking Albanian-Chinese support. If there is one undeniable characteristic of both the leadership and the rank and file of the Communist

Party, however, it is their intensive nationalism, to which ideology takes at best a second place. Who in his sane mind would assume that the road to political power in Moscow leads through Peiping and Tirana? One speech before the congress revealed Molotov's letter of October 1961 to the Central Committee, in which he allegedly criticized the new party program and assailed the current policies of revisionism and pacifism.[6] But even had Molotov written the most innocent and submissive declaration, the skilled eye of a party propagandist would still have detected in it antiparty and anti-Soviet sentiments. We must not fall into the perversity of seeing a hidden meaning or falsification in every Soviet pronouncement on recent politics, but neither can we accept their interpretation of political events without corroborating evidence.

When it comes to the reasons for the dramatic disclosures and charges at the Twenty-Second Congress, we are frankly in the realm of conjecture. Equally puzzling has been the obvious hesitation and indecision about what to do with the most culpable old Stalinists. Though several speakers at the congress declared categorically that there was no longer room in the party for Molotov, Kaganovich, and Malenkov, more than a year has elapsed (at the time of this writing) and no penalties have yet been visited upon them. But while there are no solid facts in our hands, there are clear hints as to the meaning of the drama.

On November 21, 1961, *Pravda* carried an unsigned editorial, "The Twenty-Second Congress on the Liquidation of the Consequences of the Cult of Personality." Although the article is written in the usual Pythian style, which makes its full import apparent only to the initiated, its function is obviously to dispel the various questions and criticisms which had been circulating in party circles. The first question is a basic one: why was it necessary to bring up the matter again if the Twentieth Congress in 1956 had already dealt a decisive blow to the cult of personality? No clear-cut answer is given. The party leadership, it is argued rather feebly, had to report to the congress on the progress achieved in the eradication of the cult. More interestingly, the author is at pains to deny the insinuations that the party is undergoing a crisis, or that Stalin's reign meant an organic transformation or degeneration of Communism. No personality, even one as malevolent in its character and as pervasive in its power as Stalin's, could have affected the basic advance of socialism.

The really interesting and intriguing passage comes with the following admonition: "How ridiculous and pathetic now appear those who try to force an open door *and cry that one should undertake to enrich the theory . . .*" [7] The theory is being enriched by the party program, it is explained, and by the process of socialist construction. In conclusion, the editorial emphasizes that the party should not decline but, on the contrary, grow in importance during the period of construction of Communism, and, though the party condemns the cult of personality, it does not repudiate the legitimate authority of its leaders.

The article clearly assumes that there are no domestic critics of de-Stalinization, but only those people who bring up the common-sense question of why it is necessary once again to wash dirty linen in public. But most of the argument is addressed to a second group of critics: foreign and domestic Communists who are beginning to have "doubts"—those who ask whether Stalinism was really an accident stemming from the personality of the tyrant, or whether it was a logical outcome of certain organic features of the Soviet system. It is these Communists who demand an "enrichment" of theory, that is, such organic revisions of theory and system which once and for all would prevent a return of the hideous past.

It is good to rid our minds of certain Western preconceptions. We should not read into the proponents of "enrichment of theory" the intention of transforming the Soviet Union into a democracy or of instituting a government of laws rather than of party. But the reference in the article would be meaningless unless it were being addressed to a sizable group of influential Communists in Russia and abroad to whom both the pace and the character of de-Stalinization since 1953 have been insufficient. A faction opposing them undoubtedly exists, but let us not call Stalinist, or still more absurdly proponents of the Chinese view, those who have felt that enough had been done to denounce the errors and crimes of the past and that any further discussion, any further penalties meted out to the already defeated and discredited men, could result only in harm to the system as a whole.

Like the Homeric warriors who struggled so fiercely over the possession of bodies of their fallen comrades, the rival factions have been fighting over dead men (that is, Stalin) or dead reputations. But the real issue at stake is very much alive.

Communist Party propaganda is always designed to reassure the outsider about the unbreakable and monolithic unity of the leadership. It is therefore almost impossible to identify Kremlin personalities associated with different points of view and policies. Some Western commentators have displayed a great deal of ingenuity, if not inventiveness, in spotting the alleged leaders of the "Chinese" or the "pro-Khrushchev" factions. Mikhail Suslov, for example, for years has enjoyed the reputation of a "dour ideologue" and a guardian of Communist orthodoxy; the only apparent reason for this is his gaunt physique, so different from the stereotype of the short and corpulent Communist leader. Fortunately, we find more reliable if not very extensive clues in the speeches at the congress and in recent party history.

Although the condemnation of the antiparty group was a prescribed recitation for every speaker, there was considerable variation in the tone of the attacks. The denunciation of

Molotov by Mikoyan is, for instance, cold and unemotional. Compare it to the speech by a representative of the younger generation of party leadership Shelepin, who appeared at the congress as the supervisor of the secret police (afterward he was promoted to a party secretaryship). Shelepin was ferocious in his denunciations: it is from his lips that the congress learned that Beria murdered a high official of the Armenian party, and that Stalin and Kaganovich scribbled unrepeatable obscenities on a humble petition for mercy by a distinguished military leader. The leitmotif of Shelepin's outburst was the question of how "those people" can sleep nights without the lamentations and curses of widows and orphans ringing in their ears.[8] The vehemence of this younger man contrasts tellingly with the reserve of the older leader, who had been a close collaborator of the men now denounced. It is not too fanciful to assume that the main impetus for continuing the flood of revelations about Stalinism comes from a younger group of party functionaries, men in their thirties and forties who could not have been too intimately involved in the terroristic policies of the Stalin era. It is quite understandable why they should press for the full truth about a man whom they had been taught to worship in their youth and demand an accounting from the survivors of Stalin's oligarchs. How else can one explain the humiliations administered to eighty-year-old Voroshilov, certainly no longer a person of any political significance? But apart from emotional reasons, there must be elements of political calculation. After all, the party and the state are still officered in many cases by people who had risen under Stalin, even though their positions are not of first-rank importance. What better way of embarrassing and pushing out the older leaders and getting promotions for the younger ones than by hammering at the past? And it is not inconceivable that it is among the younger and aspiring men that the voices are heard about an enrichment of theory and practice which will bar forever a return to the evils of the past.

It is interesting to speculate on Khrushchev's own position in this tug of war. No one at the congress could have been unaware of the fact that the First Secretary and Mikoyan had been persons of the highest importance in Stalin's entourage. There were feeble and probably mendacious attempts to picture Khrushchev as defying Stalin's wrath during his last years and protecting the Ukrainians from Kaganovich's depredations. It is unlikely that any of the oratory implied a criticism of the First Secretary who, through a series of cunning maneuvers, has managed to establish the popular picture of himself as the man leading Russia from the terror and inefficiency of the past. But the logic of his position must make Khrushchev the arbitrator and referee between the two factions, and not, as it is widely and rather foolishly assumed in the West, the leader of the "liberal" group. He cannot for all his dictatorial powers alienate the rising generation of the leaders; nor can he allow the denunciation of the cult of personality to turn into a critique of the whole rationale of totalitarianism. Again his performance at the congress is illuminating. Having unleashed the flood of criticism against Stalin and the antiparty group, he was eager in his concluding address both to justify the reopening of the old wounds and to indicate the permissible limits of the debate. Thus only on the last day of the congress did Khrushchev mention what, in Communist eyes, would be the gravest charge against Stalin: he referred somewhat incoherently to the mysterious circumstances surrounding the death of Kirov in 1934 and, though he did not quite say so (investigations are still proceeding), left a clear implication that the assassination was engineered by the tyrant himself. In the same speech, he recalled his assurance to Kaganovich in 1957 that the defeated faction would not be dealt with in the manner of the thirties and forties, and he asked for indulgence for old Voroshilov in view of his services to the Soviet people.[9] "Look"—Khrushchev seems to be saying—"we had to do this, for you cannot bury such horrible crimes in oblivion, but don't go too far with your cries for the blood of the old Stalinists."

Another ambiguity concerning Khrushchev's position arises from the frequent turnover of the highest party personnel. The fact is that Khrushchev's Presidium has been even less stable than Stalin's Politburo was (except during the most intense period of the great purge in the late thirties). Four of the full members added since 1957, and presumably they were the First Secretary's favorites picked by him from the relative obscurity of the provincial apparatus, were demoted at the last congress. Even earlier, Alexei Kirichenko, once reputed to be very close to Khrushchev, had been abruptly dismissed. Kirichenko came under fire at the Central Committee meeting of January 1961 for his inefficient handling of the harvest in the Ukraine in 1956.[10] But, if administrative efficiency was the goal, how can one explain that he not only continued as Khrushchev's close collaborator but was even promoted to the Central Secretariat following 1956, and that Kalchenko, to whom Khrushchev was also particularly rude, had continued for five more years as prime minister of the Ukraine and an alternate Presidium member? That the alleged past transgression could not have been the main reason for Kirichenko's fall is even more strongly suggested by Khrushchev's equal rudeness, and for the same reason of crop mismanagement, to Podgorny, the current party leader in the Ukraine.[11] Yet Podgorny was allowed to remain in his position and on the Presidium, and at the Twenty-Second Congress he was praised for the much better harvest of 1961.

A similar excuse, poor handling of crops, this time in 1959 and in Kazakhstan, was given for firing Belyayev in 1960, and yet he was succeeded as the local first secretary by Kunayev, who as prime minister of the republic must have been almost as responsible for the failures in agriculture as his predecessor. What of Aristov, Furtseva, Mukhitdinov, and Ignatov, who were dropped from the Presidium at the Twenty-Second Congress but who were retained on the Central Committee? Their demotion might have been connected with administrative failings—such as Furtseva's apparently inept handling of some policies in the Ministry of Culture, or Mukhitdinov's inability to prevent scandals in the party organizations of the Central Asian republics which were his domain—but this is unlikely to have been the whole story.

Khrushchev's style of governing, with its constant improvisations and shifts of policies and inspection tours reminiscent of the medieval monarch's, must place a heavy burden upon his subordinates. His age increases the probability that there must be maneuvers and intrigues in anticipation of the problem of succession. The First Secretary, no matter how absolute his power, can rule only with the help of a devoted elite of party officials. It may appear bizarre to an American reader that a dictator has to conciliate factions or balance generations and personalities in his entourage, but the Twenty-Second Party Congress makes this conjecture very convincing.

II

The closing of the congress was signalized by a symbolic gesture: the unveiling of the statue of Karl Marx. The story of the monument has an irony of its own. It was in 1920 that the cornerstone was laid by Lenin. The intervening years were evidently too filled up with the erection of statues to Lenin and Stalin, not to mention secondary heroes of Communism, to allow the completion of the memorial to the father of the movement. The Twenty-Second Congress was called upon to sanction a new party program which would guide the Soviet people to the threshold of Communism—hence the hasty completion of the long-forgotten project.

The setting of the ceremony enhanced the unconscious irony of the occasion. The two speakers joining Khrushchev in the unveiling were the leaders of the Communist parties of the two countries where Marx had spent his life, John Gollan of England and Walter Ulbricht of Germany. Their presence emphasized the paradox of the history of Marxism: England, where the founder's logic required that Marxism should prevail first of all countries, the actual laboratory as he thought of his system, has today an insignificant and unpopular Communist party. Its representative's speech at the congress in all probability aroused less interest than the speeches of the representatives of Communism from Syria or Peru. And Ulbricht epitomizes the fact that at least in Europe, if Communism "increaseth and waxeth still brighter," the reason lies not in its appeal to the proletariat but in the enormous power of the Soviet Union standing behind it. The paradox of contemporary Communism—its waning appeal in the industrialized countries of the West and its continuing expansion not because of any "inherent contradiction of capitalism" but largely because of the great military potential of the USSR—was well symbolized by the successive appearances of Khrushchev, Ulbricht, and Gollan and their eulogies of the founder.

The erection of the monument was designed also to emphasize the unity of Communism as a world movement. But in fact the Twenty-Second Congress could provide but little comfort to those who visualize the future of Communism as that of a united world movement or who assume that its final victory will put an end to the era of wars and national rivalries. The leadership of the Communist Party of the Soviet Union used the platform of the congress to denounce in the most categorical terms the Albanian Communists. The Russian accusations were dutifully echoed by the representatives of the great majority of the fraternal parties. But the head of the Chinese delegation, Chou En-lai, openly defied the Soviet excommunication of the Albanian leaders. For the first time since 1925, the head of the Russian Communist Party was publicly criticized from the floor of a congress: "Open onesided judgment against any fraternal Party does not favor unity and conciliation. We cannot consider an open discussion of a breach [between the two Communist parties] as a serious Marxist-Leninist approach." [12]

The Sino-Soviet differences which have been smoldering since 1956, if not before, were thus brought into the open. There could be little doubt in the mind of those present that Albania has served as a convenient outlet through which the Chinese and Russian Communist leaders could vent their mutual irritation and seek support from the leaders of other parties. Among the Asian Communists there was an understandable reluctance to challenge the Chinese viewpoint and a corresponding tendency to pass over Albania in silence.

The clash between China and the Soviet Union has several dimensions. Officially the Communist Party is engaged, as always, in combating the revisionists on the right and the dogmatists and sectarians on the left. About the revisionists, Tito's Yugoslav Communists, Khrushchev had very little to say at the congress, and the reprimand administered to them was unusually mild when contrasted with the tone used for the Albanians. The grave charges used against the latter were a little incoherent: they were accused of persisting in the Stalinist practices and of abusing the leadership of the Russian party for its denunciation of Stalinism. Chou En-lai, by undertaking the defense of the Liliputian Communist state, ranged himself in the camp of the dogmatists and sectarians, and, as was expected, the violence of his attack upon the Yugoslav revisionists was only surpassed by the tone of his references to the United States. Chou's remarks expressed fury over the fact that the Albanian Communists, who until the time of the congress had remained within the Communist bloc (not that they had had much choice), were being assailed by the Russians in terms infinitely more violent and threatening than the Yugoslavs, who had been pursuing independent polices since 1948 and had been the recipients of substantial Western help.

The intrinsic importance of Albania is practically nil. If the leaders of this Communist Ruritania have felt able during the last few years to act at first intransigently and then insolently toward the Russians, it has only been because of obvious Chinese encouragement. In the dimension of revisionism versus dogmatism, and one is forced reluctantly to employ these horrible Communist semantics (what would Eduard Bernstein, the most democratic of men, think of a classification which would consign him to the same revisionist camp as a totalitarian dictatorship?), the Chinese preference is clearly on the side designated as dogmatist. This denotes a more militant and dynamic brand of Communism than Khrushchev's party is at present willing to sponsor. Revisionism of the Yugoslav type represents to Mao and his associates a horrible specter of what the Soviet Union may become—a regime still Communist in its ideology but not militant in its propagation, indulging in extensive cultural and economic interchange with the capitalist West, willing to acknowledge at times that the individual or a social organization may have a sphere of autonomous activity. It is unlikely that the top Chinese Communists entertain undue reverence for Stalin's memory. Had the old despot lived on a few more years, his intolerance of the slightest insubordination within the Communist camp could have led to a far more drastic clash than the present one. But the continuing attack upon Stalin is perceived by the Chinese to contain also an oblique criticism of the tenets and policies they have pursued during the past five years. Now that the Russians have managed to build their country into a great industrial and military power, they can afford, so many Asian Communists would argue, to put a more humane gloss on their Communism and to wax indignant about the human sacrifices of the past. But to the Communists in the more backward countries, the detailed critique of Stalinism must have appeared almost as condescending advice not to be in such a hurry to industrialize and build a modern military machine, and to leave the defense and the direction of world Communism exclusively in the hands of the Soviet Union.

The other dimension of the conflict touches on the policies to be pursued on the world scene. Chinese impatience to reach the status of a power on a scale comparable to that of the United States and the Soviet Union is accompanied by a not unreasonable suspicion that to their Russian colleagues the prospect is far from welcome. Speaking of relations with the United States, Foreign Minister Gromyko said: "If only our two countries united their forces for the protection of peace, who would dare and who would be in a position to threaten peace. Nobody! There is no such power in the world." [13] The Communist mind is an extremely suspicious one. To Peiping, for all the realization that Gromyko's phrase was part of the standard Soviet cajolery, it must have been disturbing. The general tone of the speeches at the congress was very anti-American, and Gromyko's speech was almost exceptional in its friendly and unthreatening character. But the Chinese might not have been unmindful of the Eighteenth Party Congress in 1939 where, amidst all the defiance of Hitler's Germany and denunciations of fascism, Stalin dropped a seemingly casual remark about not "pulling anybody else's chestnuts out of the fire"; within a few months the whole pattern of Soviet foreign policy was altered.

The parallel is obviously a far-fetched one. But both Peiping and Moscow must be approaching the realization that the old pattern of relations between the USSR and world Communism is gone forever. As long as the USSR was the only Communist state in the world, there was a clear and unambiguous identity between the interests of world Communism and the Soviet national interest. But can the latter be served by the growth of another Communist state into a world power? Soviet foreign policy has already lost that freedom of action which characterized it in Stalin's day and which accounted for so many of its successes. In the Chinese view, the resources of the Soviet Union ought to serve the cause of world Communism. The Western camp, led by the United States, repeatedly has shown its weakness; hence it would be immoral as well as illogical not to exploit this weakness by more militant Communist policies.

The Chinese attitude has, then, three discernible elements. There is first of all an undoubted element of missionary zeal and militancy. In many ways the Chinese Communists are at the beginning of the road which the Soviets have already traversed. Their confidence in Communism as the wave of the future is still unbounded. In the second place, their victory in China cannot be complete as long as the United States protects Chiang Kai-shek's state on Formosa. A period of real peaceful coexistence between the United States and Russia would, at the least, postpone the realization of their minimal goal, that of reclamation of all Chinese territory, and perhaps even threaten the Mainland regime itself. That the Russians have not deployed themselves more energetically on behalf of Chinese territorial interests must be a source of profound grievance to Peiping. Similar points may be made about Chinese Communist membership in the United Nations.

But the most fundamental element in the Chinese prodding of the Russians toward a more militant posture is the fear that any, even a temporary, accommodation with the West, any determination on the part of the Soviets to leave the expansion of Communism to "historical forces" rather than to aggressive policies which hover on the brink of war, might eventually mean such a drastic alteration of the Soviet regime that the prospects of world Communism, and with them the hopes of the Chinese, would suffer an irreparable blow.

How does the same problem look from Moscow? One does not have to accept the extravagant notion of a "pro-Chinese" faction in the Soviet hierarchy to believe that there are many Soviet Communists who are genuinely worried about the internal as well as external consequences of a definite break with China. For people of Khrushchev's age and temperament, it is probably impossible to admit, even to themselves, that the moment has come when the interests of the USSR and those of world Communism have begun to diverge, and that China's achievement of the status of a great power would be a triumph for the latter and yet a grave danger to the Soviet state. What would become of the universalist pretensions of Communist ideology if it were fully realized and stated that the very victories of the movement breed tensions and create rival imperialisms that dwarf similar phenomena in the capitalist world?

It would not be too fanciful to assume that Soviet hopes for the international developments of the next five or ten years project a gradual rather than a drastic decline in Western power, accompanied by the inability of China to reach the status of a great power and, hence, her continued need for Soviet help and guidance. The Russians feel, and it is difficult to quarrel with them on this ground, that in the nature of things the social and political forces being unleashed in the underdeveloped areas of the world work for them rather than for their Western rivals. Whatever setbacks their policies have experienced, whether through confrontation of local Communists by a strong nationalist leadership (as in Egypt) or through a policing action by the United Nations (as in the Congo), the Soviet leaders remain serene in their conviction that in the longer run democratic institutions are simply not feasible under primitive economic conditions, and that the non-Communist national leaders will prove unable to satisfy the aspirations and quell the discontent of their peoples. Neutralism and anticolonialism, which in time turn into a more intimate connection with the Communist bloc, these are the pleasant prospects before Khrushchev and his associates as they contemplate the vast areas of the world. Why then attempt to speed up the tempo of expansion and risk a nuclear holocaust?

If Khrushchev seems in some cases, in Berlin or Cuba, to have appropriated Dulles' "brinkmanship," he has not been backward in developing his own version of containment. The capitalist world has no right, indeed no effective means, of preventing its gradual decay. "Liberation wars," a term which does *not* include phenomena like the Hungarian revolution, push the West out of one strategic position after another. Direct use of Soviet power is threatened only if the West attempts to reverse the trend and recoup its position. Hence we have the vague threats over Cuba and, most notably, the pressure over Berlin. The latter of course is directed against the dangerous possibility of an effective economic and political unification of Western Europe.

The above catalogue represents not unfairly what Khrushchev understands by peaceful coexistence: the safe and (mostly) peaceful expansion of Communist influence, and ultimately of Communism itself. The Chinese call for a more resolute and militant policy springs not so much from a basic rejection of the Soviet meaning of peaceful coexistence—it is unlikely that the Chinese in their sober unboastful moments desire a nuclear war or are confident that it would not topple their regime—as from a conviction that the capitalist world is much weaker and more willing to beat a retreat than their Soviet colleagues postulate, and from the suspicion that in time peaceful coexistence might become a reality.

Given the premises of both sides, it is impossible to see how the Sino-Soviet conflict can be resolved. The Soviet Union will simply not submerge its own national interest and follow the policies urged by China. The weaker position of the Chinese might for a time make them acquiesce in Soviet policies, but they are bound to resume the dispute. Nor is it possible rationally to see how either side could afford a complete break on the order of the Soviet-Yugoslav clash in 1948. China is much too weak to risk a complete isolation in world politics. As a state, the Soviet Union could easily afford the breach, but not as a *Communist* state.

It is illuminating in this context to recall a previous drastic shift in Soviet foreign policy, the Soviet-German Pact of 1939. A comparison of the situation then with the possible consequences of a sharp anti-Chinese turn now brings out the vast changes which have occurred both in world Communism and in the structure of Soviet totalitarianism. World Communism in 1939 was a monolithic movement whose principal tenet and unifying link was blind obedience to Moscow. The pact brought cries of anguish from fellow travelers and a momentary hesitation within a few Communist parties. But, apart from the effect on some relatively few individuals, the movement survived very well what seemed to be a basic betrayal of its ideology.

Nor were there any adverse repercussions in the Communist Party of the Soviet Union or in Soviet society. Both were within the iron grip of Stalin's dictatorship. It would be laughable to suppose that the dictator's position was threatened or challenged by the shift. Even if the grip of despotism had been less firm, it is still unlikely that a large number of Russian Communists would have concluded that the Nazi-Soviet Pact revealed the bankruptcy of their ideology. There was, to repeat, at that time a widespread belief at home and abroad that what was good for the Soviet Union was good for the cause of world Communism. To a Soviet Communist who tried to rationalize the sufferings of the past ten years, of the era of collectivization and the great purge, Communism could still represent the only road to industrialization and to the status of a great power, the only road to Russia's greatness.

Today a fiat from Moscow will no longer evoke the same

slavish reaction from the whole Communist world. It is worthy of note that even Stalin's quarrel with little Yugoslavia, and Khrushchev's denunciation of Stalinism in 1956, had wider reverberations in the Communist world than this ideologically much more shocking alliance with a fascist power. Postwar Communism, by its very successes, by the conquest of so many countries, has created a variety of views and interests which simply did not exist within the lean and unprosperous movement before 1939. To be sure, in any definite clash with China, the majority of Communist parties outside of Asia would line up on the Russian side, as they are right now in the present and limited phase of the conflict. But this fact could not obscure the impact of the blow that would be struck to the idea of Communism as a viable world system, and it could not, at the very least, prevent a manifold multiplication of the doubts and dissensions which have gripped the Communist world since de-Stalinization.

What effect would the clash have in the Soviet Union? The Soviet citizen today, even if he is a faithful Communist, has no overwhelming reason to believe that the future greatness of his country is bound up with ideology, which to him begins to sound more and more artificial and detached from his daily cares and concerns. The party is conscious of the growth of what might be called ideological agnosticism and spares no effort to combat it and to revive ideological fervor. But its efforts are hampered and made pathetic because it is not "opposition" that it is struggling against, but simply indifference. It is not the remnants of capitalist mentality, as is officially alleged, that the party is fighting, but, horrible to say, the beginnings of bourgeois mentality induced by the whole postwar development of Soviet society. An additional dose of disillusionment, which a sharp conflict with China would provide, would go very far in exposing the hollowness and irrelevance of the whole ideological structure.

The long-range implications of a definite break with the Chinese Communists must be joined in the minds of the Soviet leaders with apprehension about its immediate consequences. There can be little doubt that the current Soviet posture vis-à-vis China is popular within the party and in the country at large, as is every policy wherein ideological considerations take an inferior place to Soviet nationalism. But a more drastic break could hardly take place without serious repercussions at the highest party levels. It is not that the malcontents would endorse the Chinese views or that they would be less fervent in their nationalism. But such a step would be taken as evidence of blundering on the part of those responsible for it—of their inability to prevent a situation of grave danger to Communism abroad and the party at home.

Soviet foreign policy thus faces not one but two problems of coexistence. One concerns relations with the West, where the problem of coexistence means the devising and carrying out of policies which shrink the West's sphere of influence, and expand Russia's, without risking an all-out war. The problem of coexistence within the Communist bloc is even more difficult; it means the preservation of Soviet hegemony, and the ability to restrain those policies of Communist China which would involve the Soviet Union in danger, and yet avoid a definite break between the two Communist giants. If the Soviet leaders feel that "the forces of history," that is, time, are definitely on their side insofar as the first type of coexistence is concerned, it is unlikely that they delude themselves into believing that the same is true in the second case. The Chinese problem will grow, no matter what reconciliations and declarations of the "unbreakable solidarity of the socialist camp" take place in the immediate future. From the congress platform Khrushchev conjured up the danger to the Soviet Union of "German revanchism" and of the rearmed Bundeswehr.[14] But whatever fear still exists in Russia of Western Germany, a nation of some sixty million people, it was the deeper if un-spoken apprehension of China which appeared to hang over most of the congress deliberations and to mar the triumphant predictions of the future of Communism.

III

Ostensibly, the main task of the Twenty-Second Congress was to discuss and vote upon the new program of the party. In fact, the Chinese issue, the vehemence of the attack upon Stalinism and the antiparty group, pushed the program into the background. The great volume of speeches and articles devoted to the program, with all its eulogies to the enormous economic progress attained, could not obscure the fact that the attention of the world was riveted to the more sensational developments of immediate importance rather than to the rapturous descriptions of what the Soviet Union was to become by 1980.

The program was designed to fill in the growing ideological vacuum in which Soviet Communism has increasingly found itself in recent years. The new declarations purport to set guideposts for the future and to inspire the Soviet people with new enthusiasm in the building of a Communist society. A cursory comparison of the current party program with its predecessors offers a good illustration of the ideological attrition of Soviet Communism. The 1903 program of the Russian Social Democratic Workers' Party breathed an authentic revo-lutionary and socialist spirit in which the various branches of Russian socialism, including the Bolsheviks, proposed to com-bat the tsarist autocracy. The 1919 program was voted by the Bolsheviks after their seizure of power and sketched out a vision of industrialized and socialist Russia. On both occa-sions there was vigorous debate and controversy about various disputed parts of the pronouncement, even though by 1919 the Bolsheviks, having eliminated their various rivals within

Russian socialism, were well on the way to becoming a totalitarian and monolithic party.

By comparison, the 1961 document is, insofar as its political part is concerned, pallid and insubstantial. Wherever it departs from the statistics of the projected growth in consumption and production, the program becomes vague. But the vista of the productive expansion it sketches is truly impressive: by 1980 the Soviet Union is to produce 250 million tons of steel, with corresponding increases in other branches of industry. Somewhat less impressive is the projected growth in the production of the consumer goods and in the standard of living. By 1980 there is to be over a threefold increase in the latter which, though such comparisons are extremely difficult to make, would assure the Soviet citizen of a level roughly equivalent to that enjoyed today by an American.* It is superfluous to count the number of times the Soviet leaders depart from the canon of Marxism, but it is clearly against Marxist logic that the standard of living in an era of full socialism should grow more slowly than industrial production.

But what of the political and social changes which will accompany the surge of productive forces on the road to Communism? Here the language of precision and statistics disappears. We have lyrical but vague promises of the growth of social cooperation, that spontaneous initiative will replace various elements of compulsion and state supervision, but there is nothing concrete. The state and the party will still be with us in 1980, since the final extinction of the state requires the proper "internal conditions—construction of a fully developed Communist society—and external conditions—the final resolution of the contradictions between capitalism and communism on the international scene in favor of communism." [15] What,

* More specifically, while industrial production is to increase sixfold in twenty years, the workers' real wages are to rise from three to three and a half times; the peasants', more than four times; the technical intelligentsia's, "considerably." *Pravda,* July 18, 1961.

an irreverent critic might have asked following the Twenty-Second Congress, of the final resolution of the contradictions *within* Communism?

The program is an eloquent testimony of how little in any concrete political or social sense Communism has to offer the Soviet people. Its authors could not, even from a distance of twenty years, point toward a single institutional change which would make the Soviet citizen freer, more of an arbiter of his own life and less of a subject of continuous prodding and control by the party. When the Yugoslav Communists wanted to emphasize their difference from Stalinism, they instituted a system of workers' councils to share in management. It is debatable how far this institution has changed the basic facts of economic centralization and totalitarian control, but it still stands as a concrete concession to the idea of wider participation of the people in determining their own lives. But the authors of the Soviet program found themselves quite unable to devise or project a similarly modest alteration of their totalitarian structure.

One might well ask how realistic it is to assume that there is a widespread popular desire for a basic alteration in the Soviet system. It is no doubt fatuous to believe that the present generation of Russians could have an appreciation or strong desires for such exotic, from the point of view of Soviet history, institutions as the untrammeled freedoms of press and speech, a multi-party system, and so on. Everything we know points to the fact that a vast majority of the Soviet people accept the present regime as one of the facts of life and that, having destroyed the excesses of Stalinism and raised the standard of living, the government enjoys a greater measure of popularity and acceptance than any of its predecessors since November 1917. It is also unrealistic for us in the West to take an isolated case of a writer's rebellious poem, or of restlessness among a group of students or intellectuals, as evidence of a far-reaching desire for democracy as we understand it. If there are people in the Soviet Union who dream of a basic change, they cannot be very numerous. To a great majority of the population, the vision of a better future does not go beyond an improvement in the material conditions of life and a final obliteration of Stalinism, by which it is understood that the regime, while remaining totalitarian, will grow more humane and tolerant.

The preceding argument is subject to two important qualifications. First, although it is ridiculous to think that the Russian masses long for a two-party system, it is both condescending and unjust to infer that long indoctrination and suppression has entirely stifled the desire for a freer life, that there is no irritation with an existence controlled by an oligarchic bureaucracy which can order a thaw or an era of renewed vigilance. The very process of de-Stalinization is an attempt, and a clever one, to persuade the Soviet citizen that the root of his past sufferings was the criminal personality of one man and his entourage rather than the system under which he still lives.

In the second place, while for the present there is every indication of popular contentment with the regime and incredulity about any alternative to party rule, what warrants the belief that the situation will not change materially in ten or fifteen years? The present Soviet generation is the first to gather modest rewards for the years of suffering and deprivation, for the horrors of forced collectivization, purges, and war. An improved standard of living, a modicum of "socialist legality," must appear to them as the answer to their most secret prayers of ten or twenty years ago. But continued improvement must, in the nature of things, bring aspirations not only for the necessities of life but also for its luxuries, including a freer society.

It would be unprofitable to discuss this question, since it is of such a hypothetical character, except that in a strange way it is already an issue in Soviet politics. Democratic politicians, and this is their virtue as well as their weakness, can seldom think in very general terms. They have to think of public opinion and elections. The Soviet leaders, with their gigantic schemes of social engineering, are forced to take a much longer view. Their Marxist training prevents them from trusting to the accidental or fortuitous solution of a difficulty. They are forced to think of society in its totality, of every new development in the field of the arts, economics, or science as having potentially horrifying as well as benevolent consequences for politics. De-Stalinization has meant a considerable relaxation of pressures in many spheres of activity, but it has not meant, and when this comes it will mean that Russia has taken a major step toward democracy, that the party has become disinterested or less intrusive in any area of social or intellectual activity. The example of agriculture is particularly instructive and pathetic in this respect. In the last five or so years, the party—and here Khrushchev has been personally identified with the policy—has tried to finish with the rigid and harmful centralization of economic administration which characterized the Stalin era and to bestow more power and initiative upon the local administrator. But no sooner has this admirable principle been put into effect than Khrushchev, in a series of flying visits from Minsk to Vladivostok, began to lay down the most minutely detailed rules on how local administrators were to use their new power and what crops, methods of cultivation, and such, were permissible. And it was not long before chastisement, demotions, and dismissals followed the "wrong" applications of the new freedom. The party is like an overanxious parent: eager that his children acquire new responsibilities and liberties as they grow up, but terribly insistent that they exercise them in the right way.

What distinguishes the Twenty-Second Congress from its predecessors in the heyday of Stalin's despotism is, among other things, a discernible growth of apprehension about social and intellectual trends. Stalin's congresses radiated vulgar but real optimism. The whole of Soviet society was represented as marching united and joyously forward. Those who impeded the march were the Trotskyites, Bukharinites, and other traitors and "wreckers," and the source of their behavior was not any social trend but simply treason and crime. It is quite a different note which is struck by the then secretary of the Moscow district and now member of the Secretariat of the Central Committee, Demichev, when at the Twenty-Second Congress he discusses certain undesirable intellectual trends:

The Party always stresses that the political and aesthetic education of the people is being carried out in the process of an uncompromising struggle with the noxious bourgeois influence. It is even more intolerable against the background of the successes of our literature and art and our rich spiritual life that individual immature writers, artists, and composers—*from among the youth, as a rule*—suffer from such illnesses as pseudo-innovationism and formalism in art. True, they are a paltry few, *but if an illness is not nipped in the bud, it can become dangerous.* In several works of our painters, the Soviet man is purposely pictured as being coarse. They give him traits of spiritual primitivism and gloomy aestheticism. An odd combination of colors and shadows and bizarre rhymes and sounds prevent certain creative workers from seeing progressive emaciation, hopelessness, and the ideological devastation of contemporary bourgeois culture . . . The most surprising thing is that some distinguished artists, scientists, and men of letters, in fear of being considered old-fashioned, are making advances to such "seekers of the new" and imitating them.[16]

Demichiv's outburst is perhaps characteristic of the way in which some party bureaucrats view the stirrings in art and literature. The closest the congress came to a debate was precisely in talking about the new trends in literature. Demichev's attack upon pseudo-innovationism was echoed at greater length by the literary bureaucrats, Kochetov and Gribachev. They were answered tactfully by Alexander Tvardovsky, who, while joining in the paeans of praise for the party and emphasizing the need for literature to portray the heroism of Soviet man, still poked fun at the excesses of socialist realism. Tvardovsky, a distinguished Soviet poet, has in recent years gained most renown as the editor of *Novyi mir,* a literary magazine which, amidst a mass of perfectly orthodox literature, occasionally manages to publish a short story or an article which comes close to being a critique of totalitarianism.[17]

Now much of the Western comment on the recent developments in Soviet art and literature has tended both to exaggerate its "oppositionist" character and to be naive in judging the consequences. The Soviet regime is not going to collapse because a young poet alludes to anti-Semitism in his poem or because some artists paint clandestinely in the nonobjective style. Nor are the innovators rebels or would-be rebels. Tvardovsky, who was elected at the congress an alternate member of the Central Committee, obviously believes that Communism can afford writing which is not stilted and which is free from the idiotic conventions of socialist realism. Yevtushenko gives free rein to the exuberance of youth and his longing for the romantic type of literary Communism à la Mayakovsky, rather than the dreary formulas laid down by the literary bureaucrats. The fact that their activities are tolerated, despite the obviously divided opinion in party circles as to how far such people should be allowed to go, proves that, at least to some regime notables, Tvardovsky's editorial tolerance and Yevtushenko's occasional jarring poetical note are gestures of no great political significance; indeed, they may be considered a safety valve for the tensions released by de-Stalinization.

But the other side of the coin is the Soviet leaders' realization that today's isolated literary outbursts may become tomorrow's intellectual style. Russian history abounds in examples of the intellectuals' discontent providing the spark for movements of social protest. "If an illness is not nipped in the bud, it can become dangerous." What makes people like Demichev particularly irritable is their recognition that the "illness" they are dealing with is created by the very conditions of Soviet life. It is an unconvincing commonplace to assert that the artist's rejection of the stale conventions of socialist realism is evidence of the remnants of a bourgeois or capitalist spirit. On the contrary, pseudo-innovationism, or whatever one calls it, is grounded in the post-Stalin realities of Soviet life; it is an attempt, as yet apolitical and fairly isolated, to shake off the dead hand of official ideology.

"Unfortunately, we still get shallow and worthless books, ideologically and artistically barren pictures, and films which do not measure up to the lofty calling of Soviet art," said a party official of even higher eminence than Demichev.[18] Again, we have the curious insistence that this is a receding trend and that the thirst for the new and different will be a short-lived infection. It is highly characteristic that the party has found it easier to condemn and to dissociate itself from the crimes committed by Stalin and his associates than to undo the ravages of Stalinism in art and literature. The party bureaucrats seem genuinely baffled about why the relaxation following the tyrant's death has not been followed by a yet greater devotion of the artist to the party and the ideology, and why, on the contrary, there have been demands for more freedom. Some in their puzzlement reverted to the hackneyed theme that the erring writers have "isolated themselves from life" by living in Moscow or Leningrad rather than following the Soviet man in his victorious struggle on the collective farm and in the factory. But at times, as in the case of Pasternak, that puzzlement turns to dull rage, for at its bottom there is the suspicion that the forces of history do not always operate in accordance with the ideology and the party ukases.

To a Western reader, the cultural debate of the congress has an exceedingly exotic flavor. We live in a society where it is not obligatory to absorb capitalist realism or to adhere to the spirit of the *Reader's Digest* or the *Saturday Evening Post*. A canvas by Jackson Pollock does not become subject of a speech by Kennedy, and a reissue of *Lady Chatterly's Lover* does not call forth a statement from Macmillan. But the party's cultural preoccupations do not stem from whimsy or the obscurantism of individual leaders. It must be galling to spend upwards of forty years in trying to make the new Soviet man, only to find that as soon as this new man is entrusted with a bit of freedom he begins to show some startlingly individualistic traits.

Poetry and parasitism do not have much in common, despite the suspicion to the contrary which both a staunch capitalist and a staunch Communist bureaucrat might entertain. But the recent moves by the Soviet state against "social parasites" and speculators demonstrate no less than its cultural policy does that, for all its conscious desire to liberalize laws and political mores, a Communist regime has to be an Indian giver, moderating or taking away concessions if the consequences run against its premises. If for Demichev there are "still" worthless books and poems being written, then in the words of the decree of the Presidium of the Supreme Soviet of the RSFSR of May 4, 1961, "there are still individuals who are stubbornly opposed to honest work" and who "engage in forbidden businesses, private enterprise . . . derive unearned income from the exploitation of personal automobiles . . . obtain unearned income from dacha and land plots . . . build houses and dachas with funds obtained by nonlabor means . . ." [19] The decree proceeded to enact drastic measures to deal with these social derelicts: they became subject to deportation from their communities for periods of two to five years and to forced labor. Other legislation adopted at the same time called for even more draconic penalties, including death, for crimes against state property and illegal currency transactions.

On the surface, the legislation is simply witness to the fact that the USSR, like many other modern states, suffers from the phenomena of social parasitism and juvenile delinquency. One ought not to ape those Marxist theorists who see in crime under capitalism a primitive form of social protest. But the rise of the undesirable social behavior which the Soviet legislation is designed to curtail is enhanced by two fairly recent developments: the abatement of the extreme terror which had prevailed under Stalin and the rise in the standard of living. The latter creates needs and desires in society, such as for private automobiles, which the government in its paternalistic wisdom does not deem proper. Some of the crimes specified by the decrees are in fact legal rights guaranteed by the Soviet codes. It fell to Shelepin at the Twenty-Second Congress to remind his audience that the Soviet civil code still provided for the obsolescent right of private citizens to organize industrial and trade enterprises, a testimony of how important written law is regarded even in the era of socialist legality.[20] But when Shelepin waxed indignant about the codes' blessings on the right of private property and the right to use hired labor, he was speaking not against the dead letter of the law but against fairly widespread and accepted practices. No government of a modern industrialized country can forgo material incentives. In this respect, the Soviet regime is like a dog chasing its tail; it is simply impossible to find a middle ground between the egalitarian injunctions of socialism and the realities of life in a modern industrialized community. It is instructive to see Shelepin, a rising Soviet bureaucrat (after the congress he was transferred from the secret police to the central party secretariat), declaring in all seriousness that "the time has come to enact legislation providing for the punishment of the manifestations of a bureaucratic attitude." [21] In that remark is contained the whole tragicomedy of totalitarianism's effort to express itself as a government of laws rather than of men.

The short adverb *still* is the key to the wistful mood in which the Soviet leaders conceive and project their long-range plans. For all the euphoria in which they proclaim their plans for Communism in twenty years, for all their allusions to the wonderful and peaceful world when Communism as a political system will have finally triumphed, they must be half-aware that their very triumphs and successes have created a Soviet Union and a world in which the old prescriptions and solutions are losing their validity. It is not that in their own country they are struggling against the obsolescent remnants of capitalist and bourgeois mentality; they are fighting the ideological agnosticism and the as yet nonviolent aspirations for a more abundant and less harrassed life, aspirations brought in large measure by the material achievements of the Soviet years. In world affairs the greatest apprehension is not aroused by capitalism and its threat to the Soviet Union. What the Russians persist in calling capitalism, the main Western powers, has long since adopted a defensive attitude, and the West's brand of liberalism and mixed economy has, at least for the time being, lost its proselytizing ability. The immediate threat of war from the capitalist quarter would come, as the Soviet leaders realize despite their protestations, only if they miscalculate the extent and the means of their pressures upon the retreating West. A problem much more ominous—because it is ultimately insoluble, in terms of their present-day position—is posed for the Russians by the victory of Communism in China, the imposition of this industry-craving and power-hungry system upon a huge country with a population three times that of the USSR.

There is no formula of Stalin's which Khrushchev has denounced more often or with greater vehemence than the old tyrant's saying that, the closer one gets to socialism, the sharper becomes the character of the class struggle. To those in Stalin's environment who were forced to participate in his atrocities, while dreaming of a less cruel if equally Communist and authoritarian society, those words must have sounded as a gross libel on their ideology, an invitation to greater and greater human sacrifices as the social and economic goals of socialism grew closer. We might paraphrase Stalin's statement and say that, the closer the Soviet regime gets to its aim of industrialization and world-wide influence, the more vulnerable appear the basic premises of Marxism-Leninism. It is not so much the fact that the regime at any given point faces a crisis, over Berlin, the Chinese, or agriculture. Crisis is the normal condition of life for a totalitarian regime. It seldom rests content to stand still, and its continuous demands upon its citizens, its expansionist ambitions, and its struggle against the forces of life which negate the strictures of dogma cannot but generate one crisis after another. No sooner was the Twenty-Second Congress over than the summons went out for the Central Committee meeting in March to discuss the perennial Soviet problem of agriculture. But the real crisis, which must become deepened with time, is that of Marxism. The function of an ideology for a believer is to provide a convincing picture of the world and to soften the inconsistencies and cruelties of life with the inspiration of a better future. And in the world of nuclear weapons, with widening rifts in the Communist bloc and the growing middle-class aspirations of the Soviet people, it becomes increasingly difficult for the ideology to provide sure answers and to serve as the rationale for totalitarianism.

If today Communism appears to increase and wax still brighter and more glorious, it does so because of the reflected power of the Soviet Union, and not because of the inherent appeal of a doctrine which has passed its heyday.

NOTES | INDEX

NOTES

1. The Historical Role of Marxism and the Soviet System

1. Arthur Redford, *Labour Migration in England, 1800–50* (Manchester, 1926), p. 18 (italics added).
2. *Ibid.*, p. 35.
3. *A Handbook of Marxism*, Emile Burns, ed. (London, 1936), p. 25.
4. *Ibid.*, p. 26.
5. *Ibid.*, p. 27.
6. *Ibid.*, pp. 30–31.
7. *Ibid.*, pp. 38–41.
8. *Ibid.*, pp. 26, 27.
9. *Ibid.*, p. 28.
10. G. D. H. Cole, *Marxism and Anarchism, 1850–1890* (London, 1954), p. 230.
11. Isaac Deutscher, *Russia: What Next?* (New York, 1953), p. 19 (italics added).
12. V. I. Lenin, *What Is To Be Done?* (New York, 1929), pp. 32–33.
13. *Ibid.*, p. 60.
14. *Ibid.*, p. 73.
15. Sir John Maynard, *The Russian Peasant and Other Studies* (London, 1942), p. 67.
16. Merle Fainsod, *How Russia Is Ruled* (Cambridge, Mass., 1953), p. 443.
17. Barrington Moore, Jr., *Terror and Progress USSR* (Cambridge, Mass., 1954), p. 18.
18. Stalin, "Economic Problems of Socialism in the U.S.S.R.," in *Current Soviet Policies*, I, Leo Gruliow, ed. (New York, 1953), 1 (italics added).
19. *Ibid.*, p. 2.
20. Moore, p. 71.

21. Stalin, p. 3.
22. Fainsod, p. 457.

2. Stalin and the Theory of Totalitarianism

1. The same type of analysis emerges clearly from Trotsky's *History of the Russian Revolution*.

2. *XV Konferentsiya vsesoyuznoi kommunisticheskoi partii (b), stenograficheskii otchet* (Fifteenth Conference of the All-Union Communist Party, Stenographic Report; Moscow, 1927), p. 562.

3. *XIV Syezd vsesoyuznoi kommunisticheskoi partii (b), stenograficheskii otchet* (Fourteenth Congress; Moscow-Leningrad, 1926), p. 274.

4. *XV Syezd vsesoyuznoi kommunisticheskoi partii (b), stenograficheskii otchet* (Fifteenth Congress; Moscow-Leningrad, 1928), p. 256.

5. *XV Konferentsiya*, pp. 437, 456.
6. *Ibid.*, p. 601.
7. *Ibid.*, p. 721.
8. *Ibid.*, p. 749.
9. *XIV Syezd*, pp. 20–21.
10. *Ibid.*, p. 506.
11. *Ibid.*, p. 504.
12. *Ibid.*, p. 397.
13. *Ibid.*, p. 110.

14. *XVI Syezd vsesoyuznoi kommunisticheskoi partii (b), stenograficheskii otchet* (Sixteenth Congress; 2nd ed., Moscow-Leningrad, 1931), p. 291.

15. *Ibid.*, p. 292.
16. *XV Syezd*, p. 358.
17. Stalin, *Sochineniya* (Works; Moscow, 1951), XIII, 355.
18. *Ibid.*, pp. 84–112.
19. *Ibid.*, p. 259.
20. Stalin, *Ekonomicheskie problemy sotsializma v SSSR* (Moscow, 1952).
21. *Ibid.*, p. 10.

3. Soviet Ideology and Soviet Foreign Policy

1. John Foster Dulles in a letter to *The New Statesman*, February 8, 1958.

2. John Plamenatz, *German Marxism and Russian Communism* (London, 1954), pp. 350–351.

3. This interpretation is presented in Chapter One, in this volume. See also my *Unfinished Revolution* (New York, 1960).

4. George F. Kennan, "The Sources of Soviet Conduct," reprinted in *American Diplomacy, 1900–1950* (Chicago, 1951), p. 123.

5. *Ibid.*, p. 124.

6. From Khrushchev's report to the Twentieth Party Congress: "As far back as on the eve of the great October revolution, V. I. Lenin wrote 'All nations will arrive at socialism—this is inevitable—but not all

will do so in exactly the same way.' . . . Historical experience has fully confirmed this brilliant precept of Lenin's . . . In the Federal People's Republic of Yugoslavia, where power belongs to the working people and society is founded on public ownership of the means of production, unique specific forms of economic management and organization of the state apparatus are arising in the process of socialist construction." *Current Soviet Policies*, II, Leo Gruliow, ed. (New York, 1957), 37–38.

7. "The July plenary session of the Central Committee studied in detail the reasons for the development of conflict with Yugoslavia. It was a shameful role that Stalin played there. The 'Yugoslav affair' contained no problems that could not have been solved through Party discussions among comrades . . . No matter how much or how little Stalin shook not only his little finger but everything else that he could shake, Tito did not fall. Why? The reason was that in this case of disagreement with the Yugoslav comrades, Tito had behind him a state and a people who had gone through a severe school of fighting for liberty and independence, a people who gave support to their leaders." Quoted in *ibid.*, p. 183.

8. The satellite parties were told in 1953–1954 that the office of secretary general could no longer be combined with that of president or prime minister. In Imre Nagy's statement, which appears well authenticated, he mentions the discussion of Malenkov, Molotov, and Khrushchev with the Hungarian leaders in May 1953, which was designed among other things to end Rakosi's absolute domination of Hungarian Communism: "Comrade Khrushchev noted 'the matter involved was that the leadership of the Party and the state should not be concentrated in the hands of one man or a few men, this is not desirable.'" Nagy, *On Communism, in Defense of the New Course* (New York, 1957), p. 250.

9. Although there was general agreement on the over-all character of domestic reforms and the shift in foreign tactics, the pace and methods of the modification of Stalinism were the subject of considerable maneuvering within the Soviet elite. Thus the fall of Beria in the summer of 1953 was not unconnected, it is safe to say, with his attempt to claim the main credit for the alleged return to "socialist legality" and more liberal nationality policies. Malenkov's fall from the premiership was expedited by the other leaders' alarm over his identification with the policy of increased consumer goods. In addition to administrative and party intrigues, the struggle for power in the USSR has consisted during the last several years in each faction's claiming credit for the more liberal policies—policies on which all of them in principle were agreed.

10. Adam B. Ulam, *Titoism and the Cominform* (Cambridge, Mass., 1952), p. 68.

11. See Khrushchev's speech, quoted in *Current Soviet Policies*, II, 177.

4. The New Face of Soviet Totalitarianism

1. *Plenum TsK KPSS 15–19 dekabra 1958, stenograficheskii otchet* (Plenum of the Central Committee of the CPSU, December 15–19, 1958, Stenographic Report; Moscow, 1958). The practice of publishing minutes of the plenary meetings of the Central Committee is now very likely to

become the rule rather than the exception. Thus, we have the minutes of the June 1959 plenum (concerned largely with problems of automation and industrial development), and the more interesting plenum of December 1959 has also been published.

2. *Ibid.*, p. 232.

3. *Ibid.*, p. 234.

4. *Ibid.*, p. 13 (italics added).

5. *Ibid.* One pood equals 36.11 pounds.

6. *Ibid.*, p. 12. State reserves apparently had to be used during 1959 in view of the unfavorable harvest.

7. The plenum took place on September 3, 1953. The decisions were reported in *Pravda* on September 13, and Khrushchev's report was published on September 15, in the same place.

8. *Plenum 1958*, p. 41 (italics added).

9. *Ibid.* (italics added).

10. Stalin, "Economic Problems of Socialism in the U.S.S.R.," quoted in *Current Soviet Policies*, I, Leo Gruliow, ed. (New York, 1953), 19.

11. After several bumper crops, 1959 was a disappointing year in Soviet agriculture and particular troubles appeared in Kazakhstan.

12. *Plenum 1958*, p. 337.

13. *Ibid.*, p. 340.

14. *Vneocherednoi 21 syezd kommunisticheskoi partii Sovetskovo Soyuza, stenograficheskii otchet* (The Extraordinary Twenty-First Congress of the Communist Party of the Soviet Union, Stenographic Report; 2 vols., Moscow, 1959). Pervukhin's speech and recantation, II, 140–143; Saburov's speech, II, 289–292.

15. *Istoriya kommunisticheskoi partii Sovetskovo Soyuza* (History of the CPSU; Moscow, 1959). The list of those who supported Khrushchev does *not* include Voroshilov; see p. 655.

16. *Ibid.*, p. 657.

17. *Vneocherednoi 21 syezd*, II, 21.

18. *Ibid.*, I, 103 (italics added).

19. *Ibid.*, I, 105.

20. *Ibid.*, I, 107.

21. *Pravda*, December 29, 1959.

22. Speech by Polyansky reported in *Pravda*, December 23, 1959.

5. Nationalism, Panslavism, Communism

1. S. M. Soloviev, *Sobranie sochinenii* (Collected Works; St. Petersburg, n.d.), p. 3.

2. See Michael B. Petrovich, *The Emergence of Russian Panslavism, 1856–1870* (New York, 1956).

3. B. Pelikan, quoted in *Soyuz russkovo naroda* (Union of the Russian People; Moscow, 1929), pp. 250–251.

4. S. D. Sazonov, *Vospominaniya* (Memoirs; Paris, 1927), p. 338.

5. Leon Trotsky, *The Third International after Lenin* (New York, 1936), p. 30.

6. *Ibid.*, p. 61.

7. *XV Konferentsiya vsesoyuznoi kommunisticheskoi partii (b)*, (Fifteenth Conference of the All-Union CP; Moscow, 1927), p. 456.

8. This point is developed at greater length in my *Unfinished Revolution* (New York, 1960), pp. 196–250.

9. A severe criticism of Stalin, from the point of view of the present regime, for his disregard of warnings, is contained in *Istoriya kommunisticheskoi partii Sovetskovo Soyuza* (History of the CPSU; Moscow, 1959), p. 519.

10. See Herbert Feis, *Between War and Peace* (Princeton, 1960), pp. 112–116.

11. George Kennan, "The Sources of Soviet Conduct," reprinted in *American Diplomacy, 1900–1950* (Chicago, 1951), pp. 127–128.

12. Stalin, "Economic Problems of Socialism in the U.S.S.R.," in *Current Soviet Policies*, I, Leo Gruliow, ed. (New York, 1953), 7.

6. Socialism in Current Soviet Historiography

1. *Voprosy istorii* (Problems of History), March 1957, p. 4.

2. *Ibid.*, p. 13.

3. *Ibid.*, March 1955, p. 5.

4. Z. M. Bograd, reviewing G. Kostomarov's *Moskovskii sovet v 1905 godu* (The Moscow Soviet in 1905), in *ibid.*, March 1956.

5. *Ibid.*, p. 159.

6. *Ibid.*, p. 162.

7. Nasirin, "O nekotorykh voprosakh sotsialisticheskovo preobrazovaniya promyshlennosti v SSSR," *Voprosy istorii*, May 1956.

8. *Ibid.*, p. 92.

9. *Ibid.*, p. 98.

10. *Istoriya kommunisticheskoi partii Sovetskovo Soyuza* (History of the CPSU; Moscow, 1959), p. 254.

11. E. N. Burdzhalov, "O taktike bolshevikov v marte-aprele 1917 goda" (About the Tactics of the Bolsheviks in March–April 1917), *Voprosy istorii*, April 1956, p. 41.

12. *Ibid.*, p. 46.

13. In 1956, some of the missing records of the Bolsheviks' Central Committee meetings in 1917 reappeared mysteriously in the Institute of Marxism-Leninism. See *Voprosy istorii*, August 1956, p. 110.

14. Rozhov, "Programma chartistkovo konventa 1851 goda," *ibid.*, February 1957, p. 116.

15. The author, as is common in such cases, takes out insurance: he mentions Lenin's interpretation of Marx's "peaceful and legal" statement according to which it applied to the England of the nineteenth century, then a *pure* capitalist country, but not to the twentieth century, when English capitalism became entrenched behind bureaucracy and militarism. *Ibid.*, p. 117.

16. E. P. Kandel, "Iskazheniye istorii borby Marksa i Engelsa za proletarskuyu partiyu v rabotakh nekotorykh pravykh sotsialistov," *Voprosy istorii*, May 1958.

17. *Ibid.*, p. 121.

18. *Ibid.*, p. 128.
19. *Ibid.*, p. 129.
20. B. A. Chagin, *Borba marksizma-leninizma protiv filosofskovo revizionizma v kontse XIX-nachale XX vekov* (The Struggle of Marxism-Leninism against Philosophical Revisionism at the End of the Nineteenth and Beginning of the Twentieth Century; Leningrad, 1959), p. 5.
21. *Ibid.*, p. 27.
22. *Ibid.*, p. 156.
23. A. G. Mileykovsky, ed., *Reformizm, revizionizm i problemy sovremennovo kapitalizma* (Reformism, Revisionism, and Problems of Contemporary Capitalism; Moscow, 1959), p. 9.
24. Z. K. Eggert, *Borba klassov i partii v Germanii v gody pervoi mirovoi voiny, avgust 1914–oktyabr 1917* (The Class War in Germany during the First World War, August 1917–October 1917; Moscow, 1957).
25. *Ibid.*, pp. 408–409.
26. In Mileykovsky, p. 438.
27. *Ibid.*, p. 343.
28. *Ibid.*, p. 345.
29. *Ibid.*, p. 360.
30. I. G. Kabin, "Borba SEPG protiv revizionizma, za ukrepleniye edinstva svoikh ryadov" (The Struggle of the German Socialist Unity Party against Revisionism and for Solidarity), *Voprosy istorii*, March 1959, p. 144.
31. Mileykovsky, p. 102.

7. Khrushchev and Boccaccio

1. Giovanni Boccaccio, *The Decameron* (Modern Library, New York, 1930), p. 48.
2. *Pravda*, October 18, 1961.
3. *Pravda*, October 27, 1961.
4. *Ibid.*, October 30, 1961.
5. *Ibid.*, October 27, 1961.
6. Satyukov's speech, *ibid.*
7. Italics added.
8. *Pravda*, October 27, 1961.
9. *Ibid.*, October 30, 1961.
10. *Plenum tsentralnovo komiteta kommunisticheskoi partii, 10–18 yanvarya* (Plenum of the Central Committee of the CP, January 10–18; Moscow, 1961), pp. 558–559.
11. *Ibid.*, pp. 45–46.
12. *Pravda*, October 20, 1961.
13. *Ibid.*, October 24, 1961.
14. *Ibid.*, October 18, 1961.
15. *Pravda*, July 18, 1961.
16. P. N. Demichev in *Pravda*, October 20, 1961 (italics added).
17. See "Notes on Khrushchev-Stalin Feud" by Priscilla Johnson in *The Nation*, December 9, 1961.
18. Suslov, quoted in *Pravda*, October 22, 1961.

19. From *Principal Current Soviet Labor Legislation* (Washington, 1962), p. 125.

20. *Pravda*, October 25, 1961.

21. *Ibid.*

INDEX

RUSSIAN RESEARCH CENTER STUDIES

° Publications of the Harvard Project on the Soviet Social System.
† Published jointly with the Center for International Affairs, Harvard University.
‡ Out of print.